MW01490910

the GOSPEL of a

POOR WOMAN

Catherine de Hueck Doherty

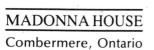

MADONNA HOUSE
Combermere, Ontario

PUBLICATIONS
Canada   K0J 1L0

Printed in Canada

Cover design: Heidi Hart

Canadian Cataloguing in Publication Data
Doherty, Catherine de Hueck, 1896-1985

The GOSPEL of a POOR WOMAN

ISBN 0-921440-27-8

1. Doherty, Catherine de Hueck, 1896-1985.
2. Christian life--Catholic authors. 3.Poor--
   Biblical teaching. I. Title.

BX2350.2.D56 1991   248.4'82   C92-090064-X

Original Publication - Dimension Books

New Canadian Edition by

Madonna House Publications
Combermere,Ont.
KOJ 1L0

Printed in Canada

TABLE OF CONTENTS

INTRODUCTION
WHY DO I WRITE
THE GOSPEL OF A POOR WOMAN?

I often ask myself in my strange vigils at night:
why *do* I want to write *The Gospel of a Poor Woman?*
What does it mean to me to be poor, to be a woman,
and to wish to write my musings, my meditations,
upon the Gospels? Frankly, it's a mystery to me.
I seem compelled to do so by some inner voice which
urges writers on.

These meditations are interwoven. I am reminded
of the beautiful necklaces I saw in Egypt when I was
small. I used to admire them — beautiful gold arti-
facts and shells. Little girls collected those necklaces
from babyhood practically. They were part of their
dowry. Pieces of gold interwoven with little shells that
seemed to have absolutely no reason for being there,
poor little things, gathered on the Mediterranean
seashore.

I think I'm writing this book because I feel shell-
like — empty. Those young people had empty shells.
If they found an interesting shell they scraped it out,
made a hole in it, and it was added to the necklace.
I have a feeling, deep down someplace, of wanting to
write *The Gospel of a Poor Woman* because I'm like a
shell, empty, and I need to be filled. I need to be filled
with the gold of God's word. Someday, I think, he will
put a necklace around my throat and it will be made
of shells filled with the gold of his words. The shells
will be filled also with his compassion, his goodness,
his love.

But above all I want to put on paper — which is absolutely stupid if you ask me — a little bit of that faith he gave me. My dear readers, tiny shells and big shells, chock full of faith, allow you to live according to his commandments. But it is to be said that he takes each shell and fills it with his words. And that's the gold that you will see on my necklace, yes, that's it: shells filled with the gold of his word. A shell is a poor thing, my friend. A shell is something children collect. Occasionally grown-ups make things with it. And hobby classes too. But a shell is a poor thing. People say, "She is a shell of a woman," or "He is a shell of a man," when they want to express that someone is dying or tired. "She looks like a shell, finely drawn, you know, transparent. She's not far from death."

Little do they know that some people are born that way. God makes them transparent. They have no education to speak of. But their souls are drawn to the Gospel, to the whole Bible. In Russia, if a young lad had some education, toward the evening when the snow was falling outside, he would read the Gospels, slowly.

Well, the Jesus Prayer stems from the Gospel. So many great spiritual works spring from the Gospel. Because after all, the Gospel is the only spiritual work that matters. It is the only teacher. I have no "education." I am very poor in that sense. If I were to go to a Bible school I'd have to start in the kindergarten to learn about the Gospel!

Well, I have a fancy that throughout the many years I have lived, God has told me a lot of things. It seems to me that I should write them down now, knowing that I am poor, which is one of the things that he told me. I really didn't have to explain that part of it. You look at him, and you look at yourself, and you know that you are poor. So I decided to write *The Gospel of a Poor Woman*. Now isn't that logical in an illogical way? It is a Gospel of one whose teacher has been God. That's all.

When I write I just think aloud, and I consider my readers friends. They are all friends, and I am sharing things with them. Maybe it's stupid, maybe it's not. Who can tell?

I have been exposed to the Gospel (I should say to the Bible) since childhood. My Father used to gather everybody together and read aloud the lesson of the day according to the Eastern Rite. Mother and all the servants would also gather to listen to the Holy Words. So, the habit of referring to the Bible, but mostly to the Gospel, has been with me since childhood, and has stayed with me until old age.

But as I read more of the Holy Book with its incredible wealth, I realized more and more my own poverty. When I was thrown on the shores of America, or I should say the new continent, the Bible was the only consolation that I had in various "brown rooms." I call them "brown rooms," those shabby boarding house rooms that I had to live in for quite a while. What else could I read at 111 Wabash Avenue when all around me people were fornicating! What else could I read in the depths of the sorrows and pain into which the Lord plunged me!

Yes, the Bible was a companion — a strange and unusual companion. I wonder if many people understand what it means. It is like a door opening. You can walk right into it — close it — and be in the midst of God's heart! The Bible speaks of the New Covenant of love. When you are down and out and haven't a friend in the world; when you stand on a corner of

Broadway and 42nd Street looking at people long-ingly, hoping that somebody would say "hello" to you, at times like these the Bible is your friend.

You go back to that brown room and what do you see? You see a door, you see a poustinia. You go in, you lock the door, and the world is yours. Truly the Kingdom of God is yours. That Book really keeps you sane. It can make you holy if you let it. Yes, it's a strange Book the Bible.

But I always read the Gospel first. The Gospel was like a voice, God speaking to me and I speaking to God, in all the brown rooms of the world that I had to live in. Yes it was beautiful. But so lonely.

You know something? This Book protects you. At least it protected me from the waters that you can see from Brooklyn Bridge. They were so enticing. And a page of that Book floated, it seemed, down before my eyes. And a voice spoke, and I left the bridge. If it hadn't been for that Book, I don't think I would have left the bridge or many other dangerous places, where near despair would have dragged me in like the undertow of the sea. There is something about the words of that holy Book that are melodious and poetic. But, as I said, I am a poor woman. It's time for me to share the Gospel according to my poverty.

ONE

GENEALOGY

The Gospel according to St. Matthew. The birth
and infancy of Jesus. Why this chapter of St. Matthew?
I don't know, except to prove that Joseph was legally
Jesus' legitimate father, and that his mother remained
a virgin. God chose well. God chose two virgins and
brought them together. God likes virginity. Why? Be
sure to ask him when you see him because he also
seems to wish people to multiply!

The Gospel begins: "Abraham was the father of
Isaac" (Matt. 1,2).* What a strange sentence. It begins
with Abraham. There were no Hebrews in the world
in those days. No, God chose a stranger.

Just imagine a very small stone, a little mountain,
not very big, a hill shall we say, and a man walking
hand in hand with his son towards the stone. Take
a look at the stone, flat, easy to sit upon. You say to
yourself, "This is a very nice nook for lovers." You
look at the shady trees that cover it and you say, "Oh,
this is a good place for a siesta in the afternoon." You
look at this flat, clean stone, and a lot of thoughts
come into your mind. It could be used for so many
purposes. It could be used to put things on when you
gather them, pigeon peas, for example. They could
put things on it because it was a long stone; it had to
be a long stone. Then you stop for a while.

The genealogy of Christ begins with a stone, but

---

*All scriptural references are to St. Matthew's Gospel unless
otherwise noted.

strangely enough it ends with wood. One of his ancestors was going to be killed because God asked Abraham the faithful one to offer his son in sacrifice. That was tough. Then God the Father asked God the Son to become incarnate, live a while amongst men, and die on a piece of wood. Isaac and Christ — stone and wood. It is good that we have a stone for our altar in which the relics of saints are enclosed. It should remind us of the genealogy of Jesus Christ. Too bad it doesn't always do that.

"Abraham was the father of Isaac, Isaac of Jacob." Jesus Christ died a real human death and rose again. By his incarnation, by his public life, his death and resurrection, he brought us together. The Sobornost of Father, Son, Holy Spirit and man was achieved. For this Christ had to shed blood.

Isaac is a symbol. Abraham was ready to sacrifice because God said so. God stopped him at the last moment. He substituted a ram. Let us think about that. Let us think about that often, again and again, for Isaac was spared, but the Son of the Father was not. Isaac had a substitute. The Son of the Father did not have a substitute. Christ is in our midst but Isaac is not. Isaac was a symbol. But he who died on the Cross and on the wood is in our midst. Did you ever stop to think about that? Every time you think of Isaac, you begin to understand how much God loved us, that he was preparing over the centuries for his Son. Beautiful isn't it?

"Isaac was the father of Jacob. Jacob the father of Judas and his brothers. Judas was the father of Perez and Zerah, Tamar being their mother," and down the line, the genealogy of Christ, proving that Joseph was his legal father, and showing the descent of Joseph from David. If Christ had had no human genealogy, that would have been terrible.

Eddie, my husband, wrote a very interesting book about the love of Joseph and Mary and their virginity. I often meditated on that virginity of God. God likes virginity. He loves virginity. I wondered why. Why, having put into man such a tremendous desire for the other sex, he blessed so deeply those who accepted virginity. How did he say it: "For while some are incapable of marriage because they were born so, or were made so by men, there are others who have themselves renounced marriage for the sake of the kingdom of Heaven" (19,12). I used to meditate about this especially when I was very poor, and there was a line up of men who would pay for your food just to have a lay with you. Coming back home so hungry, I wondered why he had counseled celibacy.

Then, as time went by, especially after I married Eddie Doherty, I understood why people embrace celibacy: Because they love *Him,* not for any other reason. All other reasons are no good. For very soon God asked us to take a vow of chastity for the sake of the Madonna House **Apostolate** — which meant for his sake. We found a strange unity developing in our hearts which quenched the fires of physical desire somewhat, and eventually totally. There are certain moments in which no desire comes forth from the body because it seems as if the body is invaded by the heart — the spirit.

Speaking as a poor woman reading the Gospel, here I was a waitress, sales clerk, and machine operator. One day I had a dream. I was young. A thousand hands reached out to me, wanting to defile me. I was a very poor person, and those young hands reached out, not in view of marriage, but with a view of fornication. In the lower strata of society they are direct about that sort of thing.

It's very tiring when you are fairly pretty. You feel that you are in the mire half the time. So to get out of the mire you think, strange as it might seem, of the genealogy of God. You say to yourself, as you read St. Matthew, "He became man, yes he became man." His ancestor was Abraham. Now what did Abraham have that I needed when I was a poor woman, young, surrounded by this mire, this salaciousness, this lust — what did I need? FAITH, the faith of Abraham. So for a poor woman in a brown room, Abraham came to mean faith — Father of faith!

Joseph's Dream

By all the laws of Moses he should have put her away. Being a man of compassion, he didn't want this to happen. In some sort of a way he thought he could circumvent the direct divorce that was required by the law.

Yes, the heat of the laundry was very intense, especially on 14th St. in New York. I was put on ironing sheets, double sheets, single sheets, and the damn, constant heat that emanated from them made me feel dizzy. There are laws in big cities too. You work, or if you are old you go on relief. If you are young — and relief was in its infancy then in New York — you work. The heat must have been very much like the heat of Nazareth, but more humid. Strange that the laundry can be an island, hot and humid.

Yes, he should have rejected her, he should have followed the laws of Moses. Everybody rejects everybody else around this world. Rejection is the law of the jungle we call civilization. But he found a way. He was compassionate and so he found a way. Still sad too, for she must have been very beautiful. Then, like lightning passes through the sky so quickly that the eye barely sees it, God's word passed through the mind and ears of Joseph. Strange were the words that the lightning brought, as strange as the prophecy of Isaiah given to a long dead king: "The virgin will conceive and give birth to a son and they will call him Emmanuel, and he shall be the saviour of his people." All this in a dream. How strange.

The page of the Gospel fell out of the book (for my book was very old — all the pages always had to be fixed up) — but it fell, caressing my cheeks. Suddenly I knew. I knew something that I had never known before. Every Christian, every baptized Christian, is pregnant with Christ, and I knew that it didn't make any difference that I was so poor. It didn't make any difference that I worked in a laundry. Nothing made any difference. I too was pregnant with Christ. I too would bring him forth in due time. But my due time is every day, because I've been baptized. I've been told something that Matthew did not know. Matthew was brought up on the Old Law. It was years later that he wrote the Gospel, and understood. He did not understand it while he was walking with God. He understood it later. He understood it when he died a martyr. Joseph understood too when he woke up that he didn't need to divorce her for she was overshadowed by the Holy Spirit.

Yes, I could hear the page of the Bible fall — but the Bible wasn't there at all. I was in my brown room. I was in the laundry. Suddenly the laundry was floating on a strange breeze. It felt cool, pleasant, to be in the laundry. I couldn't understand it until I read once more the words: "The virgin will conceive and give birth to a son and they will call him Emmanuel." So, she agreed, didn't she. And strangely enough, had you been in that laundry with its heat and its noise on 14th St., New York, you would have understood that the breeze, the cool breeze and some kind of a renewal in me, came from a single word that this woman spoke: "FIAT."

Epiphany

> Jesus was born at Bethlehem in Judaea during the reign of Herod. After his birth astrologers from the east arrived in Jerusalem, asking, 'Where is the child who is born to be king of the Jews? We observed the rising of his star, and we have come to pay him homage.' (2, 1-2)

The revelation to the Gentiles. This is Epiphany. It's a very profound feast day. Already millions have walked in the wake of the Magi.

They came to make obeisance to their king because somewhere very deep in their hearts the non-Jews were awaiting him, expecting him. It was a strange affair. It always cheered me up, especially when I was lecturing on inter-racial justice and being, you might say, beaten up by eggs and tomatoes.

Just think for a moment. Three wise men from the East. One was supposed to be a Negro, and the others were Persians. Three came to worship him, multi-coloured, in a manner of speaking.

So did I worship him. So did a thousand others. I used to worship him in the crumby little storefront, with children dancing on the garbage cans amidst all the noise of Harlem. He revealed himself to the whole world on Epiphany. Oh, I know, there are all kinds of revelations of the Lord. But the first one was Epiphany. And I was there. It gave me courage. I read and read my old half-torn Testament again and again, when I was in my various brown rooms, in Harlem and elsewhere.

Don't you see. It's so obvious, so utterly obvious that those of us who have no racial prejudice were there. And I even brought gifts to him. I brought the myrrh of my works which he had placed on my lips. The frankincense of my prayers. All the gold of compassion and understanding that he had put into my heart. And I strewed it out right in front of him. He was little, but he gathered it all up, because it was all intangible. It wasn't gold, it wasn't frankincense, it was love. Even when he was little, barely born, he would put out his little hands and gather it up. It was very simple, because he was love.

I used to read on dirty floors (I tried to keep them clean, but sometimes it was very difficult to keep rented rooms or little apartments clean). I even straightened out the pages on which Epiphany was written. It was such a beautiful feast. It brought everybody together. God walked again in our midst in my little room just as he did when he came to Adam and Eve in paradise.

It's very beautiful, this Epiphany Feast. Often I was subjected to much abuse. What's a tomato? A tomato is for eating. It's not to throw at people who tell you that God came for all men, that he died for them all. But some people used tomatoes to dirty the second hand clothes that I wore. Some hurt, you know. Yet, if you really begin to think about it, it's like you catch a tomato that's hurled at you and it changes. The cucumber turns into gold, and a potato becomes frankincense. It's all very beautiful. You sit on the floor. Your Gospel page which talks about the Epiphany flutters and you have to catch it because there is a cold wind blowing. Then you sit on your haunches and read it, and the whole room changes. It's so beautiful, so exceedingly beautiful.

It tells you another thing. It tells you that God is with you and that he will show you the other way by which you can escape from the Herods of the world.

And so, when they throw potatoes, cucumbers and all that stuff at you just because you want to proclaim Epiphany, *he shows you another way.* "Come to me all you who labour and are heavily burdened and I will shelter you, I will console you." That's exactly what he does in a brown room when you return from a lecture on inter-racial justice, and behold all your clothing soiled with vegetables, and rotten eggs. You suddenly begin to realize it's Epiphany.

TWO

THE FLIGHT INTO EGYPT

Being a sales clerk was poverty in the 1920's in Canada. It was a strange time, a very strange time. "How much is this broach, Madam?" "This comes from Greece, Madam." "It will be about $3.50." Greece, Byzantium, Constantinople, Paris, London. A poor woman sells. She is poor. The pay is only $12.00 a week and she has a child.

Long ago and far away God spoke to a man, and he said, "Go to Egypt." Did he speak through his angels or his prophets or whatever? It doesn't really matter very much. Not to the poor woman who sells baubles to the rich. Strange how one can speak and yet be far away. It happens when you are in love. You can sell anything. You can do any kind of work. You can be President of the United States, I suppose. But for poor people, love stays by you while you sell. Love is your companion whatever you do. When you are a chambermaid, love consoles you.

My first love was the Book. The Old Testament predicts the coming of Christ. The New Testament talks about Christ. The Gospel was always my consolation.

"Yes, Madam, it comes from Greece. It costs $3.50." And the page of my old Book that was at home, and almost falling apart, came fluttering between me and the customer. (It always happened.) I was far away, I was far away.

The Magi left by another route.

After they had left, the angel of the Lord appeared to

Joseph in a dream and said, 'Get up, take the child and his mother and escape with them to Egypt, and stay there until I tell you; for Herod is going to search for the child to do away with him.' So Joseph rose from sleep, and taking mother and child by night he went away with them to Egypt, and there he stayed till Herod's death. This was to fulfil what the Lord had declared through the prophet: 'I called my son out of Egypt' (2, 13-15).

The broach was sold. My Gospel page fluttered between me and the customer. It was invisible to her, but very, very visible to me. For I, too, was a refugee, like Joseph, Mary and Jesus. I was thrown by the will of God onto the shores of a new land. Somewhere, someplace, he must have said to myself and Boris my husband, "Arise, and go, and stay there until I call you." He called Boris to himself.

"This broach, Madam, comes from Egypt. It costs about $10.00." Customer interferes — but nothing really interferes with the Book, nothing. The book, New and Old, is a lover. It consoles, it clarifies, helps you to live.

But I hear the cries of the children of Russia, of Germany. Do you? How many died in Auschwitz? Who has counted them? Does anybody remember Biafra? How many died there? Take a map, a world map, and find me a place where children didn't die, killed by Hitlers, or just man's inhumanity to man. Right here in Canada I remember they died because their mothers had no milk in their breasts. I remember the night in which I was led to that God-forsaken house that had no heat in it and there were seven children there. The mother was holding the baby and giving it suck, but her breasts were flat and empty, and the child was long dead. They took the mother to a mental home, and buried the child, and they gave the other children away to the Children's Aid Society or something. It was depression time.

"Yes, Madam, it's an Egyptian make." And a voice was heard across the world — not only in Ramah, sobbing out, loudly lamenting — for it was mothers named Rachel and Joan and Catherine, and all kinds of names, weeping for their children killed by the wars, in England, Germany, Lebanon, everywhere. I could hear so clearly while the little loose leaf of my Bible passed between me and the customer. "Yes, Madam." And the customer left.

John the Baptist

About that time John the Baptist appeared as a preacher in the Judaean wilderness; his theme was: 'Repent; for the kingdom of Heaven is upon you!' It is of him that the prophet Isaiah spoke when he said, 'A voice crying aloud in the wilderness, "Prepare a way for the Lord; clear a straight path for him"' (3, 1-3).

Strange how the power machines make noise. Did you ever work on power machines in a room with 40 people? All you do all day is one side of a dress. That's all. One side of a dress. But the noise of those power machines in the old days was like a thousand buzzing bees — no, a thousand is too little — a million buzzing bees. In our modern days it would be like an armada of airplanes coming to destroy a city. No dreams are possible in that noise. No thoughts remain consecutive. It's like your brain is fragmented, chopped up with a little hatchet. The noise is deafening. Suddenly you begin to understand. Technology has entered the world — railways, street cars, automobiles, airplanes, "Concords." Probably tomorrow you will make England in fifteen minutes, who can say?

Yes, a man came out of the desert. He wore a camel's hair shirt and he was girded with a leather belt. He ate locusts and honey. Locust is a plant, but it's not very nourishing. Nor was the food sold at those hot dog stands. You know the kind? They are all over the place. They always sell coffee.

When I was in that laundry and made $7.00 a week, we used to go to those little stands. You could get a hamburger for eight cents. The man who ran it said he got them from the Pennsylvania Hotel, the leftovers of rich customers. He put them through the machine. They weren't really hamburgers, because they were already cooked. But, he said, you could put a sauce over it — sort of like beef Stroganof — and smear it on your bread. Bread was cheap. The leftovers from the rich people. And this man, clad in this strange garment, cried out, "Repent, for the kingdom of heaven is close at hand." And it is of him that the prophet Isaiah said, "He was the voice crying in the wilderness, prepare the way for the Lord, make his path straight."

All day, all day the power machines. I couldn't stand them any more. I lost track of everything.

I left the power machines and I became a waitress. I was tired of the leftovers of the rich. "If I'm a waitress," I said to myself, "I can at least eat, because in restaurants there is food. It might not be what the rich eat, but there is food." Food is a very big word. This man who cried "Repent, repent, repent!" and who was preparing the way for the Lord, had fasted a long time. To abstain from food for the glory of God and the salvation of men is more than repentance. It is love that can be gathered up in a little round ball, beautiful and small, and offered every night to Our

Lady to be given to her Son who fasted so long in the desert.

Abstaining from food — to make oneself beautiful and slim, to make oneself desirable, so as to lead souls to perdition, can also be the devil's work. That too is abstinence from food.

"Yes, Madam, the salad is delicious. It's made of big thick shrimps that just arrived from the East Coast of America."

"Yes, Madam, porterhouse steak. Of course. Pardon me? What did you say? Oh. You want a special porterhouse piece for your little dog? Yes, Madam."

The kingdom of God is at hand. Does she know it? Does she know a piece of porterhouse steak would feed a child for two days? Does she know? She doesn't. And a strange anger rises in me. And I wonder if it is just or unjust anger. Then another page of my book of the New Testament gently kisses my cheek again, and all I can read in it is, "Those who show mercy will receive mercy." But the page passes too fast, and I bring the steak for the lady with the dog.

Today is my night for overtime, for serving in the evening, and that means mostly men, business men. They talk of affairs. As you serve them, you hear of mergers worth thousands, millions of dollars. They eat well, they dress well. They are the rich ones, the powerful ones. Some are judges, some are lawyers. Who am I? Just a poor woman, a waitress, serving the rich men who talk about millions. And suddenly the page of my old Bible is before me as I stand before them ready to fulfill their slightest wish (for the manager has ordered me to). And so, I look at them and at my page, which for some unaccountable reason hovers in mid-air for a moment.

When he saw many of the Pharisees and Sadducees coming for baptism he said to them: 'You vipers' brood! Who warned you to escape from the coming retribution? Then prove your repentance by the fruit it bears; and do not presume to say to yourselves, "We have Abraham for our father." I tell you that God can make children for Abraham out of these stones here. Already the axe is laid to the roots of the trees; and every tree that fails to produce good fruit is cut down and thrown on the fire.' (3, 7-10).

Suits made in England, ties made by Sulka. Everything so conservative, so rich, so elegant. The page of my New Testament has vanished. But why do I tremble so? Why are my hands so shaky as I serve them their dessert?

Jesus Is Baptised

How strange, it appears to me now, that we pay so little attention to our baptism. Birthdays are celebrated very gloriously, very humbly. So are many other events. But the baptismal days are totally omitted. How strange! Because a baptismal day is like a sacrament reflected in one's soul. Baptism is a sacrament. But you know, the baptismal waters into which we are plunged at childhood, or in middle age, or in old age, are not calm. Oh, it might be, of course, just a little baptismal font. For a very little child among the poor who can't afford to go miles to a baptismal font, it may be just a basin. But these waters are not calm at all.

Baptism is an enormous sea. It has to be, because by entering the waters he washed us from our sins. How gigantic must be the waters to wash our sins away? The water that I have been immersed in is really the water of his life and death. Sometimes I just close my eyes and let the feel of his soles go over me, for he walked on waters and his soles touched the water. He walked on the earth, and the earth still trembles with the memory of his footsteps. I really believe that he walked not only in Palestine, but in Africa, in Canada, in all the earth. There is a certain trembling going on. Like a lover expecting his beloved. He walked on our earth. There are footprints somewhere. They are hidden.

All of the things I speak of, I speak in faith. I don't know if you knew 6th Avenue in New York in the old days. It was a series of apartments and brownstone houses where you could get a menial job. It wasn't for actresses, or for anything VIP-ish. No, just for poor women like me. You could get a job as a waitress there. Of course you had to pay 10% of your salary for one month to him who gave you the job. But that was natural. That's the rip-off that the poor are always subjected to, or used to be.

Look at this rather well-burnished brass plate of all things. It says (I forget the name but let's say) "Highbottom," because the lady who ran that place was English. That is where you got a job as an upstairs or downstairs maid.

I got a job in a place like that. I was supposed to be the upstairs maid. They had a butler and they had a chauffeur, and they had a waitress. The waitress looked after the dining room. The butler polished the silver and all that sort of thing. I sort of divided my time between the upstairs and the downstairs, and I took the place of the waitress when she had her day off.

Yes — he walked on the same earth that I was walking on.

The gardener would come and say, "What does

her Royal Highness" (meaning the boss) "desire for the
beautifying of her dining room today?" "Well," I'd
say, "she's having an ambassadrix." "Well, I guess
I'll give her mums — brown mums, golden mums,
yellow mums. All kinds of mums — sounds good for
an ambassadrix." And all the servants would laugh.

He walked on this earth. My tired feet kept
walking upstairs, downstairs, upstairs, downstairs,
making beds, serving, doing dishes, and sometimes
crying in beautiful bathrooms, sitting on the seat.

Yes, he walked on this earth, but he also walked
on the water, and the word "water" was always
consoling to me. It brought me a feeling that I too
belonged to the kingdom, his kingdom, the kingdom
of God. That I was an heir just as he was, and that his
Father and the Holy Spirit were close to me. Suddenly
baptism became a most consoling thought. He had to
leave footprints on the water, just as he had to leave
footprints on the earth, just as he had to leave footprints in my heart.

It might sound funny that in a bathroom such
thoughts would come and make my tired feet light!
They were immense houses, with so many corners to
clean. Often as I went around dusting and polishing
and serving meals, pages of my old Bible would fall
between me and whatever I was doing, and I would
suddenly be full of joy because, you see, this is what
happened:

Then Jesus arrived at the Jordan from Galilee, and
came to John to be baptized by him. John tried to
dissuade him. 'Do you come to me?' he said; 'I need
rather to be baptized by you.' Jesus replied, 'Let it be
so for the present; we do well to conform in this way
with all that God requires.' John then allowed him to
come. After baptism Jesus came up out of the water

at once, and at that moment heaven opened; he saw the Spirit of God descending like a dove to alight upon him; and a voice from heaven was heard saying, 'This is my Son, my Beloved, on whom my favour rests' (3, 13-17).

I used to think in my youth that Christ was naked three times. The first time, when he was born. Everybody is naked at birth. Secondly, he was naked when he was baptised. And thirdly, he was naked when he was crucified.

I had several poverties, one was physical and the other was spiritual. In my physical poverty, which was engineered by God himself, I somehow (I did not know it then, but I know it now) identified myself with all those who were poor. (Later in life I could even identify with a lady in India who had a baby in a culvert.)

You see how one page of the Gospel consoled me, and how, in faith, things straightened out in my life. I knew forever that one of the greatest sacraments is baptism. I cannot go to Communion and receive God unless I am baptised. So I think baptism is greater than everything else because it is the door to everything else. It truly opens onto the kingdom of heaven that John the Baptist preached about. Baptism is a door that opens onto union with God. I'm simply saying that baptism is called the entry into the kingdom of God, and I call it the entry into the kingdom of love. Without it, how could I speak his love?

THREE

TEMPTATION

And so he was baptized, and his feet touched water.

> Jesus was then led away by the Spirit into the wilderness, to be tempted by the devil. For forty days and nights he fasted, and at the end of them he was famished. The tempter approached him and said, 'If you are the Son of God, tell these stones to become bread.' Jesus answered, 'Scripture says, "Man cannot live on bread alone; he lives on every word that God utters"' (4, 1-4).

This time the page was really shabby — I mean my Bible page. It was all strung together with Scotch tape. Somehow or other it got beaten up while I was moving from brown room to brown room.

Wabash Street was a strange street, but then so were all the streets of the big cities lined with cocktail lounges. But a Wabash Street can be found anywhere. For me it was in Chicago. Wabash — probably an Indian name.

I was working as a cocktail waitress. The war was on. One thing I remember: men with trembling hands, men with young hands, men with old hands, wanting to put twenty-five cents into the juke box. "Paper Doll" was the tune of the day. Everybody wanted to hear it — why I don't know. Maybe it sang of infidelity, and of the fact that women were paper dolls that you tear apart. Yes, paper dolls.

> "And he was led into the wilderness to be tempted by the devil."

There is wilderness and wilderness. For a poor woman trying to earn some money for her child, Wabash St. was truly a wilderness. Dark and dank and frightening. The dry clean air of a poustinia, or I should say of a desert, would have been so beautiful. Instead, there was the eternally humid air filled with the smell of all kinds of drinks —Cuba Libres, bourbon on ice, White Lady. Strange words, all dealing with liquor — but they really weren't drinks. They were temptations for poor people like me.

The devil asked Jesus to turn the stones into bread, into loaves, and Jesus answered: "Man does not live by bread alone, but by every word that comes from the mouth of God."

Yet, so also does a poor cocktail waitress who tries to keep her virtue intact. If she is pretty she can very easily exchange it for a car, an apartment, jewels, dresses, things like that. Can one change a diamond necklace into food? No. All these temptations were really not temptations for me. The battered page filled with Scotch tape smiled as it flew by me, because it knew that I could not be tempted by these things. Still, the Gospel was there to remind me of his love and of his Father's love.

But the devil did not stop.

> The devil then took him to the Holy City and set him on the parapet of the temple. 'If you are the Son of God,' he said, 'Throw yourself down; for Scripture says, "He will put his angels in charge of you, and they will support you in their arms, for fear you should strike your foot against a stone."' Jesus answered him, 'Scripture says again, "You are not to put the Lord your God to the test."' (4, 5-7).

Yes, that was one more time I was grateful for my parents. They never allowed me to test God. They always told me that I must be tested *by* God, but never test God. That was a very sensible teaching. So I did not want, even as Jesus did not want, to fall from all kinds of pinnacles, all kinds of ramparts. I knew that angels supported me. Angels were always around, messengers of God, sustainers, messengers of the Spirit. They were helpful in so many ways, but never, never would they be there if I doubted that the Lord was my sustainer, and that the angels who sustained me were only his messengers. That was very clear in my mind — always had been clear. So on that page of my Bible was a wet spot. Some GI had put his beer down on it and it stuck.

But the devil was persistent.

> Once again, the devil took him to a very high mountain, and showed him all the kingdoms of the world in their glory. 'All these,' he said, 'I will give you, if you will only fall down and do me homage.' But Jesus said, 'Begone, Satan! Scripture says, "You shall do homage to the Lord your God and worship him alone."' Then the devil left him; and angels appeared and waited on him (4, 8-11).

It was still while I was on Wabash St. that I met that sort of a temptation. A millionaire came into the cocktail lounge. This millionaire got interested in me and wanted to give me everything — a place in Venice, a house in New York, a flat in Paris. He wanted to marry me, but he was divorced. From the pinnacles of high mountains I beheld the opportunity of wealth of such magnitude that I couldn't fathom it even though my family had been wealthy. Somehow or other this very clean leaf fell between him and me. Very clearly I heard the voice of God saying, "Be off, Satan! For Scripture says, you shall worship the Lord your God and serve him alone."

And that's how it was. I could not worship man, the man who offered me all these gifts, or was able to give them to me. For I knew that beneath it all I could not in conscience accept his proposals. They were the devil's ways. And so I stayed on Wabash Street, a cocktail waitress who wouldn't give in. The policemen, the people on the street, the guys who dropped in to sell the wine, they all called me "Duchess" because they thought I was unapproachable. Perhaps I was, but then what can you be when the leaves of an old book, the Gospel, come between you and everything else.

A Light Has Dawned

> When he heard that John had been arrested, Jesus withdrew to Galilee; and leaving Nazareth he went and settled at Capernaum on the Sea of Galilee, in the district of Zebulun and Naphtali. This was to fulfil the passage in the prophet Isaiah which tells of 'the land of Zebulun, the land of Naphtali, the Way of the Sea, the land beyond Jordan, heathen Galilee,' and says:
>
> > "The people that lived in darkness saw a great light; light dawned on the dwellers in the land of death's dark shadow."
>
> From that day Jesus began to proclaim the message: 'Repent; for the kingdom of Heaven is upon you' (4, 12-17).

I read this in one of my brown rooms, in the evening, by a light that hung from the ceiling and had no shade. The moment he left the desert, news of his relative, in fact, the boy whom his mother helped to deliver, reached him. I said to myself, of course he would leave everything and go. He returned to Galilee upon hearing that John had been arrested.

That's how it was with me, too. How funny that

this reading of the Gospel brings back so many
memories. It was difficult during the war, I mean the
Revolution, to find out who was where at what time.
You felt so totally abandoned — your own people
turning against you. That's something nobody understands unless they have been in a civil war — brother
fighting against brother.

I knew my mother was in Finland. I knew that
they had salvaged much from the Petrograd apartment. But father vanished, and so did Serge my
brother. We couldn't find them anywhere. People like
us lived on rumours. Someone would pass you by on
the street and say "I heard . . . " and so through the
grapevine we heard that father hid himself in a big
yacht belonging to the de Hueck family. And Serge was
there too. That's all we knew. Had they found sanctuary or not we didn't know.

We had to flee and flee we did, I and Boris. But
we weren't like Christ. We didn't go "where St. John
was arrested." We couldn't, because we did not know
whether father and Serge were arrested or not. So we
went to Finland. It's funny how you can go someplace, and yet your heart is in another place. And so
we were out there in our dacha in Finland, but Boris
was worried about his mother, and I was worried
about my father and Serge.

A motor boat is passing by our window, and I was
thinking (looking at the motor boat) how many times,
how many ways, refugees — Hungarians, Russians,
Germans, Jews, Vietnamese — have escaped. Sometimes, perhaps, it would have been better had they
died, for where were they to go?

It's like the 6th Avenue I was telling you about.
I found a job. I had to pay ten percent commission
for the first week. In those days you had to have the

Bible to help you, the Gospel especially. Because what did Christ do?

Hearing that John was in prison, he went where the imprisonment took place. But from that moment Jesus began his preaching with the message, "Repent, for the kingdom of heaven is close at hand."

Now, laundry, power machines, sales clerk, cocktail waitress, all kinds of jobs blended together. Yes, the pages of my old, grubby little Gospel kept floating before my eyes. Again I heard cuba libra, bourbon on the rocks, something else on the rocks. Sometimes I didn't hear well because my mind was very far away. So I would go back and ask what it was they wanted. It was always the same thing seemingly, monotonously, like the "Paper Doll" that they always wanted to play on the juke box. I had to preach the Gospel. I had to preach the Gospel in that stinking, lousy gin-mill. That's what my Gospel told me to do. And the pages of St. Matthew just kept flickering and flickering and flickering. Yes, Christians have to preach the Gospel under all conditions: quietly or loudly, on platforms, and even in gin-mills.

I remember the day when I announced to a group of GI's and their girl friends that the place was closing. It was time — 4 o'clock, and I was off. They were laughing and joshing and having quite a lot of drinks.

"Where are you going from here, Katie?" said they. I said, "To church." You should have seen the faces of those people. They said, "To church? What's the matter with you? Are you a Catholic?" Because it was Sunday I said, "Yes, I go to St. Paul's Polish church." It was opened for people like me: low masses at 3 and 4 and 5 o'clock in the morning. They said, "We'll go with you." So they did.

It was the funniest thing. They sat in the back and

I went to Communion, and I came back, and they said, "Let's go and have a cup of coffee and some Danish." I said, "That's a very good idea." They said, "Katie, you go to Communion? And you work in a gin-mill?" And I said, "Yes, I go to Communion, and I work in a gin-mill. What difference does it make where I work." "Well," one girl said, "I am a Catholic, and that means that you haven't committed a mortal sin last week." "Well," I said, "Could you imagine that I didn't commit a mortal sin in two weeks?" "Well, in the atmosphere that you work," she said, "I can't imagine it, but it's evidently true." "Well," I said, "I better go to bed, for I have to start early." On Sundays we started at 3 PM or so. "Well," said the boys and girls (there were two girls and three boys) "that's sure a lesson I never had from any priest, or nun. Going to Communion and working in a gin-mill!"

A couple of weeks later one girl returned. She said, "You know, I was struck by that idea. I was really struck! If you can live that life, the way you live it, well, baby, so can I. To hell with all the GI's and all that — I'm going to Confession."

That's the last I saw of her. And I heard a little song as if two or three pages were rubbing together and singing along as they rubbed — the Bible pages, I mean, the Gospel.

Jesus Heals

Jesus was walking by the Sea of Galilee when he saw two brothers, Simon called Peter and his brother Andrew, casting a net into the lake; for they were fishermen. Jesus said to them, 'Come with me, and I will make you fishers of men.' And at once they left their nets and followed him. He went on, and saw another pair of brothers, James son of Zebedee and his

brother John; they were in the boat with their father
Zebedee, overhauling their nets. He called them, and
at once they left the boat and their father, and followed
him (4, 18-22).

What a strange page to come my way. Frankly it
wasn't a page — it was a piece torn from a page,
because, as I said before, I was very poor, and I had
a very poor Gospel. By poor I mean old, and the pages
were all held together by Scotch tape. I had brought
it from Russia. Or did I? No. I brought it from Finland.
Strangely enough, it was an English Gospel. I was
wondering why it was an English Gospel and then I
remembered that at one time long before the Revolution, I was studying the English Holy Words. They
are not the same as in Russian, so I was trying to
figure out how the Russian and the English Gospel
compared.

It reminded me of the early days of our Apostolate.
All along the line, I had wanted to sell all that I
possessed, take up my cross and follow him. Well,
factually, that is what the first disciples did. Because
they had done it, I wanted to do it too. And above all,
even now, my admiration is for the speed with which
they did it. He passed. He called. They followed! And
that's the way I wanted to do it. But, of course, it
took some time.

You see, this is another thing: Peter had a wife.
Maybe he had children, but we don't know. I had a
child. Then into my heart always like a sort of a song
I heard: "Unless you leave your father, your mother,
your children, your brothers, your sisters, everything,
you are not worthy of me." And so, when I was walking
down our Toronto streets from Isabella to Portland,
I think I answered his call like his disciples! And it
warms my heart even today. That I had this, shall we

say, courage, was, of course, his grace again.

But the Gospel went on:

> He went round the whole of Galilee, teaching in the synagogues, preaching the gospel of the Kingdom, and curing whatever illness or infirmity there was among the people. His fame reached the whole of Syria; and sufferers from every kind of illness, racked with pain, possessed by devils, epileptic, or paralysed, were all brought to him, and he cured them. Great crowds also followed him, from Galilee and the Ten Towns, from Jerusalem and Judaea, and from Transjordan (4, 23-25).

How many memories of the hospitals that I worked in came back. In World War I, I dipped into the sea of pain. There was this youngster — shrapnel had hit him in the stomach. The wound was terrible. He had before him about ten miles of a difficult drive in a covered wagon (like in America) pulled by two horses. There he was among many, and he would smile and say, "Do you remember the reading in the Gospel where Christ healed? Well, I believe in what he said, and though I have a hole in my stomach, I think he will heal me." And all this because they believed. And if I believe it's perhaps because humble Russian soldiers believed, and the humiliati of which Dostoyevsky writes believed, and because of the thousands who rose to new life in the prisons of Siberia.

I'm very sad that in our time we haven't understood one simple thing which our wounded soldiers and our illiterate peasants understood. "Yes," as they all said, "he will cure us, but we must be a 'bratstvo' before he cures." That's a very interesting word "bratstvo." It means brotherhood. If you save a person from the sea or from any danger of health, if you save a person's life, you exchange crosses. Every

Russian gets a cross at baptism. Poor or rich, they get it. It might be gold or silver, or it might be copper. After a life-saving incident, both saviour and the saved exchange their crosses. That makes them brothers. They call it "brothers in the spirit." And such people are "bratstvo." The Russians understood well that you cannot cure or be cured unless you love.

God passed by the sick and the lame and the halt and the blind. And he cured them because he loved them. He had created them. He didn't mean for them to be sick. That happened because man decided to spurn God. He cured them because he loved them. And they were cured because they had faith. Faith and love are able to cure. And he always said, "Thy faith has made thee whole." But in our modern century, as the page passed me by, it wept. Do you think that a poor woman's Gospel, battered and bruised, can weep? I don't know — but it seemed as if it did.

FOUR
THE BEATITUDES

The days are sort of grey. New York is always grey in the fall toward November. I'm trying to find a job. Sixth Avenue seems far away. I really should have a warmer coat but I can't afford it. Quite suddenly, then, as my soul bemoans my poverty, a page of the Gospel passes in front of my face and disappears. And all I can catch is one sentence. But then, of course, it's part of quite a long sentence. It says on the page, "When he saw the crowds he went up the hill. There he took his seat, and when his disciples had gathered round him he began to address them. And this is the teaching he gave" (5, 1-2).

There is no hill that I can see in New York. It is drizzling. Crowds, yes, there are lots of crowds. But his voice comes at me out of the page loud and clear: "How happy are the poor in spirit; theirs is the kingdom of heaven." Well, when your coat is very thin, the distinction between reality and spirit is difficult to make. What did he mean, "poor in spirit"? Well, I turned left when I should have turned right toward 6th Ave. But I was bemused, intrigued by this strange sentence. "Blessed are the poor in spirit; theirs is the kingdom of heaven." Then I remembered. Yes, the ones who do not desire anything except God, who become poor for his sake or accept poverty for his sake, and therefore rejoice in their poverty, are full of his spirit, yes. Something like that.

I shivered in my thin coat, and my heart began to be glad because I came a little closer to what he said long ago and far away. The sun was shining and the grass was green in Palestine. He went on, for the page came back: "Happy the gentle; they shall have the earth for their heritage." Well, there used to be another way of saying it in my old Bible, but anyhow, this was old too, and it said: "Happy the gentle; they shall have the earth for their inheritance." The gentle. Hmmmm.

I turned into another street which seemed to be leading me away from 6th Avenue where I could get a job. But I was fascinated with all those pages the wind hurled at me, but they weren't hurled at me. They were just making soft funny sounds like the rain and snowflakes that fall like rain and die on the pavement. Gentle. "Happy are the gentle, they shall have the earth for their heritage." That took me a long time to absorb. What does it mean? What did it mean to a poor woman in a shabby coat wandering the streets of New York? Oh, I understood. It meant a gentleness of heart. To put it bluntly and simply, it pertained to the same words that he spoke before: love your neighbour as yourself. If you love, you are gentle.

So I connected the two, and I asked myself if I was gentle. Well, frankly, it is difficult to be gentle when you are poor. You first have to acquire the spirit of poverty that he was talking about, the acceptance of poverty if you are poor, and the non-desiring of things if you are rich. Then you begin to love your neighbour. You become gentle. Was I gentle to the last waitress? I wondered. I was mad because she swiped my tip. I wasn't gentle at all. I was rough. I used all kinds of bad words to ball her out. She was sorry. She gave me back those pennies. It was only ten or fifteen cents. And she had a child. She was working very hard. I had a child too. No, I wasn't gentle.

Suddenly my heart was filled with great sorrow,

and I listened to my heart weep. Did you ever listen
to your heart weep? It's quite an experience. It weeps
like the rain. Not heavy. No. It splashes like a drop
against the window. Have you ever been young
enough to look at a raindrop splashing at your window
and wonder where it went to. That's how I felt. And as
I felt that way, I forgave that woman, and a great
gentleness and love toward her sprang in my heart.
I went back, by and by, to that restaurant where she
and I worked, but she had gone, and so I could not
apologize to her. I was sorry.

But do you know that these Beatitudes are ter-
rifying when you try to live them. "Happy those who
mourn: they shall be comforted." He said, "Happy
those who hunger and thirst for what is right: they shall
be satisfied." In the old Bible the words were "for
justice." Well, "Happy those who mourn, they shall be
comforted." You know, I gave up 6th Avenue. It was
getting too rainy. I walked into a cheap restaurant
and ordered a cup of coffee, because these Beatitudes
were engulfing me, and I had to think it out, I mean,
it's no use thinking it out in the rain. And when you
have a very, very shabby coat you get wet. Poverty
bites, even when you decide you are going to be a
saint, it still bites, and it sort of dampens all ideas of
sanctity, if you know what I mean.

So I sat at this drab table with this coffee and I
thought to myself, "Happy those who mourn, they
shall be comforted." Now I'm sure it's un-theological.
I'm positive, because I had a very beautiful idea about
that but it had nothing to do with mourning dead
people. No. Happy those who mourn the state of the
world, who mourn sin. That's what he meant. I sipped
my coffee slowly. When you haven't got much money,
a cup of coffee, which at that time cost five cents, is

quite a treat. Dorothy Day and I used to go to Childs' because they used to give two cups of coffee for five cents.

So, "Happy those who mourn, they shall be comforted." Happy those who mourn for everybody, for the Hindu woman who has a baby in the culvert, for the third world and its tears, that raised some of the bananas which the first world needs. (What is the "first world" I never figured out!) I thought of all the people who work in the tropics. Sweat pours off them, and nobody mourns that stuff. Somebody has to mourn the inhumanity of man to man. Somebody has to cry out to God, "Out of the depths I cry to you. Behold, behold what they do to Thy people!" Yes, I almost made a whole psalm by myself, drinking slowly that very warm, pleasant coffee, because that was going to be my supper.

But those pages kept coming: "Happy those who hunger and thirst for what is right, they shall be satisfied." There was just myself and a cup of coffee in a shabby restaurant. I thirsted for what was right. I wanted a job, just a plain, ordinary, rightfully-belonging-to-me job. Every human being should have a job or something that enables him to eat. I thought of all the friends I had: waitresses and truck drivers, and taxi men and all kinds, and all those who hunger and thirst for what is right. They are not satisfied. So, I wondered. I don't know. There still was half a cup. I drank slowly and sipped it. But if you were a poor woman in a shabby coat, marshalling slowly a cup of warm coffee, would you be satisfied? Would you believe that justice existed? No, it doesn't. It existed for the rich, but it certainly didn't exist for the poor such as I, so I thought. I still think — I'm not sure. It's one of my temptations.

"Happy the merciful, they shall have mercy shown to them." I had no trouble with that. There was no problem at all so long as he was talking about himself. Sure, if we are merciful to others, he is going to be merciful to us. That stands to reason, because he is fair, God is. But, as the cup of coffee finished (I had put a lot of sugar into it), I said to myself, well, he will be merciful. But I must be merciful when they are not merciful. I am not always merciful, but he is always merciful.

"Happy the pure in heart: they shall see God. Happy the peacemakers: they shall be called sons of God." Oh, there was no problem at all. I applauded. My heart applauded. You can't really applaud in a restaurant, but my heart applauded. That was true. "Happy the pure of heart, they shall see God." Of course they shall see God, even before they get there. They don't have to go to heaven, they are going to see him now. This I see very clearly, so very clearly. What else could God call the peacemakers. He was the Prince of Peace. Obviously Abba, his Father, would call them sons, his own sons.

"Happy those who are persecuted in the cause of right; theirs is the kingdom of heaven. Happy are you when people abuse you and persecute you and speak all kinds of calumny against you on my account. Rejoice and be glad, for your reward will be great in heaven; this is how they persecuted the prophets before you."

Yes, sir, this made sense to me. I'd been persecuted a lot. And I was in a shabby coat drinking the last of the coffee. The persecution was, "Oh, you are a Polack, eh? Can you speak English?" And 6th Avenue was not exactly polite about it. It wasn't persecution, it was needling. Needling — the more so that the needling was done often by people who themselves were not pure Americans. But then, when I understood the Beatitudes a little better as life went on, I realized what persecution really meant. Then I rejoiced. I rejoiced remembering the cup of coffee.

The Salt and The Light

That's what he said. He said it very simply. "You are the salt of the earth. But if salt becomes tasteless, what can make it salty again? It is good for nothing, and can only be thrown out to be trampled underfoot by men" (5,13).

The night was very dark. I didn't feel like any salt at all. In fact, I felt very much as if I were the salt that should be trampled underfoot. The car was wide, the road was narrow, and each time I turned the wheel, I hit a branch. Of course I had the windows closed, but still there were branches hitting the car on both sides. When the night is dark, and the road is narrow, and branches hit you on all sides, strange sounds melt with the engine noise. You feel kind of lonely.

So here I was going to nurse somebody. They had told me the way, but I had never been there before. So I had to rely on the Lord. No, I didn't feel like salt. Not at all. I felt flat, flat, flat! The kind of salt that they give to people with heart conditions — it just doesn't taste like anything.

I lost my way. I had to return. And each time the branches hit the windows I said to myself how stupid I was. Why was I on this road, on this narrow, difficult road. For at one point it suddenly dipped, and what did I find at the end of it? Well, there was a bridge. Most unsafe. But I kind of slid into it, because the night was dark, the rain was coming on, the roads were slippery, and I didn't feel like any salt at all.

But finally I made the house, and they were so happy to see me. The woman had cancer. It had been almost 24 hours or more since she had had a shot of morphine prescribed by the doctor. I administered the shot, and I did a lot of things too long to mention. It was dawn when I left the place.

As I travelled back across the strange and dangerous bridge, across the narrow roads, with the branches still hitting the car windows, a page of my Gospel (would you believe it?) stuck to my windshield, and I had to stop and "get it off." Right there, I could read it. Yes, there it was on my windshield. (It isn't everybody who gets pages of the Gospel on their windshield!) I could read very clearly: "You are the salt of the earth. But if salt becomes tasteless, what can make it salty again? It is good for nothing, and can only be thrown out to be trampled underfoot by men."

Then the page disappeared. The windshield was clean again, clear again, you might say. I came home, I was tired, and I went to sleep, even though it was daytime. When I woke up, I took the Bible — I love to read it, you know — and it was the Gospel I always read, and strangely enough my eyes fell on the same page that stuck by my windshield. It said, "You are the light of the world. A city built on a hill-top cannot be hidden. No one lights a lamp to put it under a tub; they put in on the lamp-stand where it shines for everyone in the house. In the same way your light must shine in the sight of men, so that, seeing your good works, they may give the praise to your Father in heaven" (5, 14-16).

How can a poor woman who has no money, or very little, who is forever looking for jobs, who is a stranger in a strange land, tell me, how can she shine? I asked myself. How can she be a light to begin with?

Half of the time poor people had no kerosene. Well, they had candles of course. They were cheaper. But still, what does he mean when he said you have to be on a lamp-stand for everybody to look at you so that your works and life glorify him and his father? That's a very tough part of the Gospel, for a poor person. It's tougher, I imagine, for the rich.

Well, I had to get a job. Again 6th Avenue loomed in the offing. I tried the bus, the cheapest transportation in any part of the world. I stood by the bus stop waiting for the bus to take me to 6th Avenue. There was a little Negro woman there also, standing, leaning against the lamp-post. I walked up to her and I asked her if she was feeling well. "Oh, no," she said. She was feeling lousy. She had been waiting for the bus a long time, to go to the hospital. She looked terrible. Terrible. So I opened my purse. The hospital was not very far away. I stopped a taxi, and I put her in, and I brought her to the hospital. I turned to the taxi driver and said, "Look, I'm a very poor woman. I haven't got very much money." I opened my purse, and I said, "I can't give you a tip. I wish I could. I know you deserve it, but forgive me, I can't." You know what the taxi driver did? You would never believe it. He said, "Madam, I'll give you a tip." And he did, 25 cents, and he put the meter down. "Oh," I said, "Thank you so very much." So we got her to the hospital and she was looked after.

Of course I missed my appointment off 6th Avenue. So I came there the next day and boy, did the guy ball me out. He said, "If you want a job you should be on time. What do you think this is, a railroad station where you go in through a door and out another or something like that? If you can't keep an appointment with us, how can you keep an appointment with a job?

I give up." And on and on he went. But the poor have to be meek, you have to take it, you have to sit there and take it, and take it, and say you're sorry, and never tell them why you were late.

I got a job. One day the man who dished out the jobs and I and the taxi driver all collided, you might say, on 6th Avenue. "Oh," says the taxi driver, "The lady I gave a tip to." The other one says, "What did you say?" He says, "You don't know what a dame you've got here!" And he told the whole story of how I got this lady to the hospital. The Jewish gentleman from the office turned around and apologized. He said, "Madam," (he always called me Katie before) "I want to give you a tip too. Don't pay me the 10%." "Oh," I said, "Life is really wonderful!"

I came home and I was very happy, and I opened the Bible, and you know what I read? It's really something. You wouldn't believe it. "You are the light of the world. A city built on a hill-top cannot be hidden. No one lights a lamp to put it under a tub; they put it on the lamp-stand where it shines for everyone in the house. In the same way your light must shine in the sight of men, so that, seeing your good works, they may give the praise to your Father in Heaven." Well, don't you think that that's what happened? So it doesn't make much difference if you are poor. The Gospel is valid for the poor as well as for the rich.

The Law

I must admit it was cold. Real cold. Almost like winter, but it was still fall. I was standing in line. Did you ever stand in a soup line, or a coffee line, or a doughnut line, or the kind of a line that "charitable people" invent to give the poor enough to fill the stomach but not enough to stop the hunger?

The line was long, and into my mind suddenly fell a page of my beloved Gospel. The Gospel was always a great consolation, and, believe it or not, food for my soul. I was so terribly hungry. Right before my eyes, I read,

> Do not imagine that I have come to abolish the Law or the Prophets. I have come not to abolish but to complete them. I tell you solemnly, till heaven and earth disappear, not one dot, not one little stroke, shall disappear from the Law until its purpose is achieved. Therefore, the man who infringes even one of the least of these commandments and teaches others to do the same will be considered the least in the kingdom of heaven; but the man who keeps them and teaches them will be considered great in the kingdom of heaven (5, 17-19).

The line shuffled two steps forward. It still was cold. And I said to myself, "What's he talking about? The kind of Law that I read about in the Old Testament hadn't been fulfilled very much." But it was too cold to muse or think about the Law, and I started thinking about him. Because, if there was a fulfillment of the Law, then he was it. He was the fulfillment.

One more step — no, two more steps — we moved two more steps, and I continued my meditation. It's very difficult to meditate when you are very cold, and you are very hungry. Somehow your meditation turns into contemplation. And would you believe it or not, on such a strange thing as the Law. It's quite true, I said to myself. He was speaking the truth as usual. Listen. He makes it very clear . . . to me anyhow. Well, I have this page before me, (as I shuffle my feet to keep warm) that says he didn't come to abolish the Law or the prophets.

What did the prophets say? The prophets called for humility, patience, charity, justice, hospitality, for all kinds of things that we dream about, we who are poor and shuffling in a line for coffee or doughnuts or soup. That's what we dream about. What the prophets called the people of the Old Testament to fulfill. And so he says, very clearly, "I didn't come to abolish but to complete." Of course he came to complete. If he was in charge of this kitchen there wouldn't be a kitchen. There would be a tremendous field, and there would be fishes and loaves enough for everyone.

If you want to discuss the Mosaic Law, remember that Christ was the new Moses just as he was the new Adam, and he abolished the Mosaic Law in his very person. An eye for an eye and all the rest of it. Look, didn't he tell them that the Sabbath existed for the people, not the people for the Sabbath, and that was a Mosaic Law? Go down the line and you will find that he fulfilled what all those prophets foretold. He himself was the fulfillment of the Law and the prophets. He said that so clearly.

You know how it worked? As you came close to the kitchen there was a very well polished glass, 13 or 14 feet wide, separating the street from all those goodies that you could eat. As I looked at it, there was my page, but it was the strangest page I ever saw. Nothing was written on it, except an outline of himself — his face, his beard, his locks, his flowing robes. He passed through the windows and disappeared. And I understood what Matthew meant when he tried to explain the fulfillment of the Law to the Pharisees.

The door opened, I walked in, and was shown a bench to sit upon. Then a sour looking woman who held a tray of coffee and doughnuts came up to me and said, "So young, and already perverted." And without a single volition of mine, just as if it was he who spoke, I said, "Lady, judge not and you shall not be judged."

You know what happened? They threw me out! They decided I was no good. And the Law was not fulfilled.

FIVE
THE OLD AND THE NEW

The room was not quite brown I must admit. Somehow or other the landlady had put a little color into the wallpaper, or was it the spring sun that reflected its lights on the page? I don't know, but right in front of me was my old, old Bible. As usual I was reading the New Testament. I also like the Old Testament. I never had anything against it. But I must admit that I always felt that Jesus Christ took something old and transformed it into something new. I can't explain that, not being a theologian, but just a poor woman. I always felt he was taking the law of the Pharisees and kind of changing it. As I was reading the Bible in the evening, I had very bad ideas. Bad reactions. I said to myself, "What he said made sense." What they predicted about him, made sense. But what all those theologians and all those big shots wrote did not make sense to me, not the way they write it up. I could never understand all those big books.

Jesus went on to say, "You have learnt how it was said to our ancestors: you must not kill; and if anyone does kill he must answer for it before the court. But I say this to you: anyone who is angry with his brother will answer for it before the Sanhedrin; and if a man calls him 'Renegade' he will answer for it in hell fire. So then, if you are bringing your offering to the altar and there remember that your brother has something against you, leave your offering there before the altar, go and be reconciled with your brother first, and then come back and present your offering" (5, 20-24).

I was sitting. Did you ever look at the tables in these brown rooms? They are kitchen tables. They too are painted brown and they have four legs, at least most of them. But they are all covered with previous boarders' carvings. The desire to leave for posterity at least one sentence is in the heart of man . But come and look with me at that table. "How lonely can a big city be. Jim." "I tried to pick up a prostitute but I was too shy, and anyhow it wasn't worth it." Then of course there is all kinds of foul language. And then suddenly, in the midst of all these, there is a terrible cry, at least there was on my table: "Where is God?" And it had a long question mark, "Well, well, well," chiseled into the table.

Yes, I had to be reconciled. But are people reconciled who write on tables? You have to be reconciled first with God. Then you have to be reconciled with yourself. What is there in you to be reconciled with yourself? When you are very poor, the self is opened up. It's just like you were naked in the heart. Everybody can push you around, anybody can call you names. Because you don't amount to anything. Not in the sight of the people. When I was a dishwasher all I heard was: "What are you trying to do? Waste my time? There are customers waiting for glasses." And I was on glasses. The guy who hired me for seven dollars a week to work eight hours a day on glasses thought I was slow. Whereas I was going as fast as I could.

I remember so well when I was a cocktail waitress I was supposed to go to bed (what they call a "lay" in America) with the VIP customers. Well, a policeman was always a VIP customer. He not only got drinks and money on Wabash Street in the old days. Amongst other things he was entitled to invite

all the waitresses to his bed. So came my turn and I
decided, "All right, you have to be reconciled to your
brother. Understand that."

So when he met me outside at 3 AM I said to him
that I was hungry. So he took me to a restaurant. In
fact, I ate a very good steak with all the trimmings.
I said to him, because he was Irish, "I look at you,
and I feel so bad. Your good mother brought you up,
I'm sure, as a good Catholic." And I started telling
him what I thought of him as a man. I said, "You are
here to have a lay with me. "But," I said, "that's not
what you really want. You have a wife. Why do you
want to be unfaithful to her? What do I present to you?
Nothing interesting, just a one-night stand. Why don't
you remember your mother, your parish priest, all the
Sisters that taught you?"

Well, believe it or not, I had him crying in the
steak. "Katie," he said, "Thank you. Forget the 'lay.'
Thank you." "You know," I said, "there's something
else that you have to do. You have to go to Confession
and ask God to forgive you. Me, I forgive you." So he
gets up and kisses me on both cheeks, and pays the bill
for the apple pie and ice cream that he ordered, I was
finishing the steak. He departed.

About twenty minutes later (because the restaurant was next to St. Mary's on Wabash Street, the
Paulist Fathers' church), he returns. "I did it, Katie, I
did it. Now I'm going to my wife and I'll be happy.
Thank you." The waitresses watched all this and they
knew where I worked. Everybody watched it. They
said, "Katie, what's the matter with you, you could
have gotten a fin out of that." "Oh," I said, "I got much
more than a fin," and I meant it. All this came back to
me as I was reading this story.

Christ and Matthew go on. "You have learnt

how it was said: You must not commit adultery. But I say this to you: if a man looks at a woman lustfully, he has already committed adultery with her in his heart" (5, 27-28).

For Jesus Christ, adultery is in the heart; it is a desire to possess. As the *Struggle with God,* my beloved Russian book, says, "Poverty desires nothing, not women, donkeys, nor horses, nor any possession. of my neighbour." Lust is in the eyes, and from the eyes it goes into the heart and the heart screams at night. Screams out of sadness and sorrow, because it has been unfaithful to the Lord. And yet you carry on, even though you see so much of it in restaurants and all these places I worked in. New York is filled with adultery, and if it isn't adultery it's fornication. They live by it. Very tiresome, you know. Very tiresome, when you have so much of it.

> You have learnt how it was said: Eye for eye and tooth for tooth. But I say this to you: offer the wicked man no resistance. On the contrary, if anyone hits you on the right cheek, offer him the other as well; if a man takes you to law and would have your tunic, let him have your cloak as well. And if anyone orders you to go one mile, go two with him. Give to anyone who asks, and if anyone wants to borrow, do not turn away (5, 38-42).

That was also the Gospel of Dorothy Day. She quoted it at every lecture and at all times. And what is the most extraordinary thing, she lived it. She meant it and she lived it. I felt, as I still feel, that I have so much to learn from her. I read her books and suddenly it isn't her book at all, it is St. Matthew, St. Luke, St. John. It's the Apostles.

The Old Law said "a tooth for a tooth." But the Lord says you must "offer the wicked man no resistance."

Look at the world today. The Catholic Worker was pacifist. They lived through three wars and remained pacifists. Thanks be to God for them.

> You have learnt how it was said: You must love your neighbour and hate your enemy. But I say this to you: love your enemies and pray for those who persecute you: in this way you will be sons of your Father in heaven, for he causes his sun to rise on bad men as well as good, and his rain to fall on honest and dishonest men alike (5, 43-38).

It took a long time for my hatred of the Communists to die. I do not hate Communists any more. I hate Communism, that is, Atheistic Communism. But I don't hate Communists. I took in X who was supposed to be my worst enemy. But was she? I don't know. I nursed her and I loved her and that was that. Today, by the grace of God and his beloved Mother, I can honestly say that I love everybody. I might not like everybody, but I love them.

When I finished reading this Gospel in my brown room with a scarred desk, I just knelt down, Russian style, prostrated myself, and thanked God that, at least at that time, I didn't hate anyone.

The Secret of the King

Whenever I read spiritual books, (and I read quite a lot of spiritual books from my childhood on), and I came across the phrase "the secret of the King," I got all excited. Spiritual books are all about God. I used to get them from the library. Poor people can't afford to buy books.

These books excited me. It was as if Christ came just to me, and said, "Look, there are a few things I want to tell you; they are not exactly secrets, but you have to keep them in your heart. The less said about them the better."

> Be careful not to parade your good deeds before men
> to attract their notice; by doing this you will lose all
> reward from your Father in heaven. So when you give
> alms, do not have it trumpeted before you; this is what
> the hypocrites do in the synagogues and in the streets
> to win men's admiration. I tell you solemnly, they have
> had their reward. But when you give alms, your left
> hand must not know what your right is doing; your
> almsgiving must be secret, and your Father who sees
> all that is done in secret will reward you (6, 1-4).

I like that secret. To me that's a nice little secret.
My right hand mustn't know what my left hand does.
Think about it. Ah, I thought, some day when I am a
little richer, I will buy a new Bible. Mine is sometimes
so bad I can't read the words, they are so smudged. But
I think I read that correctly. So it made me think, it
made me think.

The church I went to had a front pew. In those
days you had to have your name put on the pew. A
family "bought" a pew and put its name on it. I forgot
the name of the persons who occupied the front pew to
the left of the aisle, but the girls who used to come
to the little Greek restaurant where I was the only
waitress used to make fun of the party that occupied
the first pew. So I said to myself, what's the matter
with them? What's so funny that they are always
laughing?

One day I saw why. She walked like a queen. She
didn't walk — she glided. She was all wrapped up —
well I shouldn't say wrapped up — she was dressed — it
was fall — in velvet, a velvet costume, the kind that
they used to call a tailored suit. There she was in green
velvet, and she had a white blouse with a jabot.
(Everybody knows what a jabot is. It's a sort of decora-
tion made of lace.) She had a lovely hat. I cannot show

it in a book, but it was very lovely. It was green velvet too and smart.

There she was. For the first time I noticed absolute silence and peace that followed in her wake.

Came time for the collection. It was a very difficult time for me because I really had nothing to put in. I always sat in the back bench, you know, at the edge of the congregation. When they passed by, all I could put in was two pennies or even less. I wasn't ashamed, but I was sad that I couldn't put in more.

This woman used to take out her very lovely velvet green purse which was bordered with a gold chain, take it out very carefully, so that everybody could see. She would open it up while the guy with the basket stood by respectfully. She would take out a $100.00 bill, open it up, and straighten it out and put it in. She didn't go to Communion though. She was the "Madam" of a bordello in one of the main towns of Canada. It was really interesting: 100 bucks from the "Madam" every Sunday, and always in the front seat, and always making a little noise to show indeed that it was a hundred dollars. After leaving the church I thought, "Poor, poor madam. You have already received your reward."

But there was something else that was a secret of the King. Reading in Matthew's Gospel, I noticed that God said again:

> And when you pray, do not imitate the hypocrites: they love to say their prayers standing up in the synagogues and at the street corners for people to see them. I tell you solemnly they have had their reward. But when you pray go to your room, close your door, and pray to your Father who is in that secret place, and your Father who sees all that is done in secret will reward you (6, 5-6).

That puzzled me quite a little bit. God said, "Pray always." Then he said, "Pray in secret." Then he says, "You cannot put your light under a bushel." Very contradictory, God is, don't you think so? I think so. Very full of contradictions.

What does he want us to do? Pray at all times, all over the place? Then I said to myself, stop. Think a little. For the secrets of the King are not secrets, and you have to have a key to them sometimes. Now a key is opening your heart and listening to what this Gospel says. So I listened again and I said to myself, well, it goes like this. God is tired of us yackety-yacking, because our prayers are all for ourselves. He doesn't mind us praying for ourselves, but not 24 hours a day, if you know what I mean. I'm sure he likes the rosary and all these prayers, but he likes the gifts people gave him in the old days, little lambs newly-born, pigeons and so forth. It was beautiful. They gave of their poverty. They gave the first fruits of their crops. And we should do the same in prayer. We should give the first fruit to God. That's what we must do. And the first fruit of our prayer is God himself. So prayer is savouring God himself: through the Bible, through the Gospel, through all his Words, through the liturgy. It's a very simple thing.

As you begin to understand that you don't pray only for yourself, you pray for him to enter your soul. I implore him that he should enter other peoples' souls. So I said to him, "Lord, please, open their doors, walk in, be part of them. I want You so much. I would like to carry You to their doorsteps and say, 'I have caught God, now I give him to you!'"

Prayer is a secret. Don't peek in. I kept thinking about it. A day shall come, so I said to myself in my youth, when I shall disappear, because I shall become a prayer, a real prayer, just as it says here. It says, "They love to say prayers so that all people will know about it." And when you become a prayer then, of course, there is no secret anymore. Then Christ and you are one and there is something that you cannot put into words. For the end of all prayer is really what I call sobornost: One person who has absorbed Christ completely, has become one with him, and gives him to another person. That is really what prayer is.

That was the secret of prayer that God really meant us to have. Of course, that meant that we weren't talking out loud all over the place. But it still happens at times that some people fold their hands, close their eyes, and look upwards so that you would think them at prayer. As soon as you go away they stop.

I used to clean St. Clare's church. There was a lady there who always interrupted me. She used to tell all kinds of stories about everybody. I invited her to clean the church because they had nobody to clean it. But she said her back was too sore. If anybody came in besides myself she immediately knelt down and looked very pious. I used to laugh. I said, "Why do you do that?" And she said, "To give good example to the children!"

He taught us how to pray. This is what he said:

In your prayers do not babble as the pagans do, for they think that by using many words they will make themselves heard. Do not be like them; your Father knows what you need before you ask him. So you should pray like this:

Our Father in heaven,
may your name be held holy,
your kingdom come,
your will be done,

on earth as in heaven.
Give us today our daily bread.
And forgive us our debts,
as we have forgiven those who are in debt to us.
And do not put us to the test,
but save us from the evil one.

Yes, if you forgive others their failings, your heavenly
Father will forgive you yours; but if you do not
forgive others, your Father will not forgive your
failings either (6, 7-15).

Well, I must admit this is a good translation. But
my Bible was very old and it went quite differently. It
said: "Our Father who art in heaven, hallowed be Thy
name, Thy kingdom come, Thy will be done on earth
as it is in heaven. Give us this day our daily bread and
forgive us our trepasses as we forgive those who
trespass against us. Lead us not into temptation, but
deliver us from evil." I like that one better, because it
encompasses everything. Yes, I like that prayer better
than the new translation. "Our Father who art in
heaven, hallowed be Thy name." This presupposes
faith. Deep, deep, deep faith. It means that we let God
do everything.

He asks also that we fast in secret.

When you fast do not put on a gloomy look as the
hypocrites do: they pull long faces to let men know
they are fasting. I tell you solemnly, they have had
their reward. But when you fast, put oil on your head
and wash your face, so that no one will know you are
fasting except your Father who sees all that is done in
secret: and your Father who sees all that is done in
secret will reward you (6, 16-18).

That's sensible. So there you are. All the good
things: fasting, praying, giving alms, must be done in
secret. These are the secrets of the King, and the Father

will see them, and he will reward you later. But I think that's only natural.

I noticed the donations of all the millionaires. I remember there was a man called Mellon. He had donated some kind of statue. Well, it took a whole page in the newspaper to tell all about it. But that statue only cost a million, and, according to the same paper, he was worth, at the time anyhow, one hundred million. I couldn't even visualize what a hundred million looked like. Anyway, the secrets of the King were very puzzling, and my old Bible curled up.

SIX

GOD AND MONEY

Once I wrote a poem, "Faites Vos Jeux, Messieurs, Mesdames, Faites Vos Jeux." It had something to do with a "croupier," the guy who dishes out the cards in a casino. He was calling out to everybody to get on with the game because time was short. And I thought to myself, "Yes, how true." Play your cards, friend, play your cards.

God deals strange cards. One card promises everything and leads to nothingness. The other promises nothing, in this world, except perhaps the kiss of Christ which is his pain and sorrow, and at the end promises joy. Strange cards, don't you think so?

The pages are really getting frayed! It says, "Do not store up treasures for yourself on earth where moth and rust destroy them and thieves break in and steal. For where your treasure is, there will be your heart also" (6, 19-21).

That is really something I can understand well. It's no problem for me to give away everything I have. That kind of poverty doesn't bother me. In fact, I don't even regret the things I give away. I'm only too happy to get rid of them.

Is that completely true? As a Catholic, as a believer, as a baptized person, is there in my heart something I don't WANT to give away? You know, this sounds like I'm proud. Maybe I am. Or arrogant. But there is another word that describes what I feel: self-satisfaction. You know that word very well. I look in my heart and I see that God has really detached me from everything. Family. Money. And now he is detaching me from the Apostolate that I'm supposed to have created at his bidding! It takes time to face that! But somehow, strangely enough, I'm facing it quite easily. It doesn't seem to bother me as much as it would have a few years ago. Am I ready to give up the Apostolate? I think I am.

Little things bother me a bit, but not much. I like to fix the donations of jewelry. I like sorting.   All those little things that don't matter to anybody. Well, that's what I like to do.

As I mediate on my old Gospel I realize what true treasures are. Yes, I do. My only tragedy is that I cannot pass that on to others. For wherever your treasure is, there your heart will be.

"The lamp of the body," says my Gospel, "is the eye. It follows that if your eye is sound your whole body will be filled with light. But if your eye is diseased, your whole body will be all darkness. If then the light inside you is darkness, what darkness that will be!" (6, 22-23)

As I read this particular paragraph I think of a blind man on a corner of a street, begging. To submit to some special law he had pencils that he supposedly sold, but I never saw anybody buying a pencil; the same amount of pencils were always there. He probably made a fair living. I used to come and talk with him. Periodically I took him for a coffee-klatch, if you know what I mean. Just coffee. It was a poor neighbourhood, and the owner always gave him a Danish.

I have never heard such a luminous explanation of the Gospel as I heard from this blind man. I remember one time he said to me, "Catherine, it's wonderful to be blind. Yes! Because you live in an entirely different world. I don't mean the world of touch or of hearing. No, you live in a world of God because your eyes are wide open to all he said and all he wants us to do. On the corner of my street I can love an awful lot of people. And I do. Especially the ones who try to steal my pennies."

We went back to his corner and for months I meditated on what he had said.

The eyes of the soul are luminous when you are blind. Perhaps especially when you are blind.

God and money. "No one can be a slave to two masters. He will either hate the first and love the second, or treat the first with respect and the second with scorn. You cannot be slaves both of God and money" (6,24).

This page of my Bible was all curled up at this point. What I had to do was an extraordinary thing. I had to take two pieces of paper and iron the thing out. I couldn't read it. Of course I knew it but you always have to read. And when I read that, my heart jumped. Jumped with a sort of strange joy! Sinner that I am, I have chosen the better part. Poverty was a goal, the goal of my life. And I finally achieved it.

But the strangest thing happened! There was a time when I had nothing and I used to beg. Oh! That was a beautiful time. Nobody depended on me and I was unknown. How good that was — how good it was! Anyhow, my heart still hungers for poverty. The real physical poverty.

"But do you know something, Lord? They have tied me with a thousand cords. Little cords mostly, but I can't move. They justify so much! Would you believe it, I'm living in a blue house and it has to be paid for? I'm travelling on some kind of plane that has to be paid for specially. Everything seems wrong somehow. Will you please listen to that Gospel of yours? See. You said it. So I've ironed it out. So it's up to You now, to let me go into a poustinia where no one knows who I am. I want to be poor. I feel sad. I love all the staff workers, but they are all children. I know that you have given me children . . . but still. They talk about poverty but they don't want it. So it seems to me. I don't know why. Probably I am all wrong, but as I read St. Matthew about God and money, what can I say? Somewhere I must be wrong."

So there is God and there is money and the eye the lamp of the body. Now I ask you — what can a poor woman do? She has no money, so she doesn't worry about it. But when you come to think of it, she has a lot to give up besides money. True, money is the source of all evil, but she can give up her will. It's not easy. No, for a poor woman it's not easy, especially for a poor woman like me with education, with this and that, and a child. No, it isn't easy to give up the thought of money.

But besides that, it isn't easy to give up one's will. To give up one's will to God is beautiful. People always wonder how to do that. Well, it's so very simple . . . very, very, simple! Suppose you were a salesman like I was in a big shop — a big emporium in New York — and the sales manager called you in and said, "Look, Catherine, you are getting the highest commissions of all. Will you tell me how? What's your secret?" I answered, "It's because I do the Will of God."

I must admit this man was very, very astonished. "What do you mean, the Will of God?" he said. "That doesn't enter into business, does it?"

"Oh," said I, "everything enters into God, even business. You and I made an agreement, but there was a third party to that agreement. Your Personnel Manager interviewed me and outlined my duties when

I became your employee. He was very clear about it. I agreed. Now comes the doing. Of course, I can escape. I can go into the toilet and smoke my cigarettes. I can go and have my coffee on any floor. There are all kinds of coffee shops. I can spend an awful lot of time chatting with other sales clerks. There are a thousand ways I can waste your money. But you see, I can't, because I made a contract between you, me, and God, and I cannot be unfaithful to it. I could be unfaithful to you, the company, but I cannot be unfaithful to God. That would be lying. I'm a Christian, and I can't lie like that."

He looked at me very seriously and said, "Catherine, evidently it pays off to be a Christian." He was a Jew. I said, "Oh yes, sir. It pays off." You understand how deep those things must go for a woman who is poor?

Trust

> That is why I am telling you not to worry about your life and what you are to eat, nor about your body and how you are to clothe it. Surely life means more than food, and the body more than clothing! Look at the birds in the sky. They do not sow or reap or gather into barns; yet your heavenly Father feeds them. Are you not worth much more than they are? (6, 25-26).

Well, I must admit that this passage is truly a joy to read for a poor woman because at least she knows that God trusts her and that she can trust God. You have to be very poor to trust God. Clothing comes to you from the Salvation Army, or somebody gives you some old rags that you can sew up and change. It's not what I'm dressed in or what I earn that matters. It's what's in my heart.

You begin to realize as you grow up that God trusts the untrustworthy. He makes the sun shine on the good and the bad. He gives harvest to the good and the bad. So why shouldn't we do likewise? Why shouldn't we trust each other? But unfortunately this is very rare.

When you're very poor, you're mistrusted automatically. You have to take slaps in the face all the time. For instance, you hire yourself for a day's work as a cleaning maid. In those days you got fifty cents for a whole day's work. That was very little money. And yet the lady who hired me wanted to see my purse before I left. She said to me, "Catherine, do you object to opening your purse? I'm not a very trustful person." I said, "No Madam, I don't object." I opened my purse and the only thing in it was a handkerchief. I added the fifty cents she had given me. She said, "You have nothing in the purse." I said, "No, Madam, I have nothing in the purse except the fifty cents that you gave me for ten hours of work." I walked out the door and gently closed it.

That's one case. Another case was being "put on the till" as we used to call it in one of the big stores like Eatons or Sears-Roebuck. I was selling magazines and newspapers. Well, that necessitates making change constantly. You punch the cash register. The drawer comes out and you have to make change and put in whatever the customer gives you. A woman comes in the morning and gives you so much money. You have to sign a receipt for it. She doesn't trust you very much but you can understand that.

At night the guy comes with a key. He always came to my till last of all. Everybody had left and here I was with him, and he was checking the till twice. I asked him why. "You are a Polack," he

answered, "and you people have to be watched."
I walked out of the store. I leaned against the wall
outside and cried. No matter what you do when you're
poor, you're always mistrusted.

I thought of God again, because right at that
moment, out of nowhere, a page of my little Bible
floated before my eyes with these very words, "Don't
worry about what you eat and drink." Walking home
(for I didn't have very much money and so couldn't
take the streetcar), with tears going down my cheeks,
I said, "Lord, how is it possible for us to really believe
what You say when nobody believes in *us?* It's awfully
difficult to believe in You when nobody believes
in me."

I turned the corner. I was living in Montreal in
those days and I had a little brown room with a French
family. I came into that house and I tried to wash away
the trace of my tears. The landlady was a gentle person
and she said in French, "Catherine, you have been
crying." "Yes, I have been crying. Nobody trusts me."
And I explained it all to her. She said, "Sweetheart,
ma cherie, nobody trusts us either. My husband and
me and the children. Nobody trusts us. We are the
poor. Everybody kicks us around. You have to
remember one thing. God trusts us. Just think about
that."

I went into my little room and thought about it.
And suddenly I realized something: God was saying
those things because he wanted us to depend totally on
himself. He revealed to me a glorious truth. I didn't
have any Friendship House in those days, nor any
Madonna House, but I understood in that little room
with the French lady in Montreal that someday I
would trust everybody, even the untrustworthy. It
was a very deep lesson, I must admit.

False Prophets

Yes, it was a lovely night. The moonlight made everything silvery as in all the novels. It was so light that I could read my Bible by moonlight. It's not every night that you can do that. It makes you think of Genesis and how God created the world. I like Genesis' story of creation much better than the scientific theories. That's probably because I have faith.

Anyhow, I read the Gospel of St. Matthew.

> Do not judge, and you will not be judged; because the judgements you give are the judgements you will get, and the amount you measure out is the amount you will be given. Why do you observe the splinter in your brother's eye and never notice the plank in your own? How dare you say to your brother 'Let me take the splinter out of your eye,' when all the time there is a plank in your own? Hypocrite! Take the plank out of your own eye first, and then you will see clearly enough to take the splinter out of your brother's eye (7, 1-5).

I thought about that! How terribly difficult it is not to judge! Here already false prophets whisper in your ears. You know what these false prophets are? I'll tell you. They are man's judgements. Relying entirely on his "brilliant intellect," man judges his neighbour according to his own standards.

One day I came across an old book dating back to 1815 or so. There was a picture in it of a father and a mother standing by a door and a girl who appeared to be pregnant. The father and mother were pointing their finger at the girl, and evidently saying to her, "Out." They judged her. They didn't have any compassion, or anything, they just threw her out. That was a false judgement.

Then I started thinking about wars. There are so

many wars that you can't keep track of them anymore. Each party thinks his judgement is right. That
is why they enter into war. But their judgement is
not right.

So, according to this paragraph of the Gospel of
St. Matthew, those who judge will be judged in turn.
Best of all, I said to myself, don't judge anybody.
That's why sometimes I don't judge even that which
is obvious. Unless it's my business to judge, I refuse
to do so. It's difficult.

The Gospel went on, "Do not profane sacred
things. Do not give dogs what is holy; and do not throw
your pearls in front of pigs, or they may trample them
and then turn on you and tear you to pieces" (7,6).

How true! Here again I could hear the whisper of
false prophets. I was not happy about so many move-
ments in the past. They grew, they mushroomed, they
disappeared, guru and all. I didn't like those false gods
that were being created for those youngsters.

As I read my old book, pages curled. It isn't so
easy to read by moonlight. Still, the letters become
very big. As if God approved of what I thought. See,
I have a tremendous gift. I have God. If I exchange
him for a thousand pieces of silver and gold, for any
idols whatsoever, for any false gods, then — Lord
help me!

Well, Matthew brought me a very effective prayer.

Ask, and it will be given to you; search, and you will
find; knock, and the door will be opened to you. For
the one who asks always receives; the one who searches
always finds; the one who knocks will always have
the door opened to him. Is there a man among you
who would hand his son a stone when he asked for
bread? Or would hand him a snake when he asked for
a fish? If you, then, who are evil, know how to give
your children what is good, how much more will your

Father in heaven give good things to those who ask
him! (7, 7-11)

Do I believe these words? I certainly do. But I
play a little game with God. I don't ask directly.
I dream about things and hand him my dreams like
other people hand him petitions.

Do you know that every dream I dreamt in him
and for him came true in Madonna House. It would
take a large book to tell you all about it. This Gospel
certainly is true.

Now Matthew talks about the golden rule. "So
always treat others as you would like them to treat
you; that is the meaning of the Law and the Prophets"
(7,12).

That is a profound thought! While I was reading
this, the moon hid itself someplace. So I began
thinking of different things. You treat others as you
wish you were treated . . . and nothing happens . . .
nothing happens! They accept, but you don't get
anything back, if you know what I mean. However,
you must continue. When you are very poor, nobody
treats you as the Gospel suggests, but that musn't stop
you from treating others as the Gospel says.

Matthew continues: "Enter by the narrow gate,
since the road that leads to perdition is wide and
spacious, and many take it; but it is a narrow gate and
a hard road that leads to life, and only a few find it"
(7, 13-14). I like that very much. Having been so
terribly poor, I didn't choose that road, but he lead me
to it, and he walked with me, so it wasn't so difficult.

SEVEN
THE TRUE DISCIPLE

It was raining, and New York rain can be very monotonous, especially in the slums where the roofs leak. Well, the landlady brought basins and all kinds of things to catch the water. I was alone and my old Bible was shriveled up from the humid air and the unceasing rain. It was that kind of a rain. Well, I opened it, rain or no rain. I like my Bible. I liked the New Testament. It consoled me.

When you have a day off from being a waitress you begin to realize how your feet swell. You know by the second-hand shoes you get from the Salvation Army (which everybody calls "Sally Ann,") that your feet are getting bigger. You start off wearing size 6½ and a year later you are wearing a size seven. Well, in my old age I've reached size 8½. It didn't matter very much, except that they just ached. You walk and you walk and you walk. How many thousand of miles do poor people walk? You walk to find a job, for you can't afford streetcars. Even in the old days, five cents was expensive. So you walk.

For some jobs, of course, you stand, but most of the time you have to walk. Upstairs maid — you walk; downstairs maid, you walk. The laundress . . . stand. Waitress . . . walk. Always you are either standing or walking. They say it's good for your feet, but the majority of the old people who are very poor have varicose veins.

Well, I opened my old book. That's a consolation. Very few people understand this tremendous consolation of the Gospel. If you are married,you can have all the children around you and tell them stories from the Gospel. If you are single, it consoles you. If you are a widow, it strengthens you. If you are married, it brings peace to both of you. It's a good thing to read the Gospel.

So there I was in my dark little room with the blub, blub, blub of those drops that fell into all those basins. And outside, a real good rain. I thought the farmers would be glad for it. I opened my book. It was Matthew. You know what God wanted to tell me on that rainy day off when I was resting my feet?

"It is not those who say to me, 'Lord, Lord,' who will enter the kingdom of heaven, but the person who does the will of my Father in heaven." That's a brilliant sentence. Of course, the Lord said a lot of brilliant sentences, but this is one of the best. I read it again and again and again. So it isn't you or I or X or Y or Z who goes around saying "Lord, Lord, Lord" who is a true disciple.

This business of praising God these days sometimes saddens me. Those who praise God have to do the will of God. But do they? When they do, I take my hat off to them. In fact, I bow low according to the way of my people. But I wonder as I bow, do they obey the Father? They should, in order to be true disciples.

In the year 1981 my Gospel is getting older and older and the pages are falling out. But in the year 1981 you would imagine that true disciples would know that: to do the will of the Father. But looking at the "communities" all over the place, you see so much of "I'm going to do what I want, when I went to do it, as I want to do it." That doesn't seem to be sufficient. There is a cacophony of voices all prophesying, all curing, all healing. It's the age of miracles. True disciples can perform miracles. He said so. He encouraged it. He said, "Go ahead, do greater miracles than I do." Who is doing the miracles? Who is moving the soul of this person to do miracles — God, the devil, or an inflated ego?

How can you tell a true disciple? He is the one who does the will of the Father.

> When the day comes many will say to me, 'Lord, Lord, did we not prophesy in your name, cast out demons in your name, work miracles in your name?' Then I shall tell them to their faces: 'I have never known you; away from me, you evil men!' (7, 22-23).

Have you ever read that sentence? I've read it often in my own Bible. It's a very strong sentence.

> Therefore, everyone who listens to these words of mine and acts on them will be like a sensible man who built his house on rock. Rain came down, floods rose, gales blew and hurled themselves against that house, and it did not fall: it was founded on rock. But everyone who listens to these words of mine and does not act on them will be like a stupid man who built his house on sand. Rain came down, floods rose, gales blew and struck that house, and it fell; and what a fall it had! (7, 24-27).

I have written in my little diary so many times about those things. A priest I knew always said, "By their fruits you shall know them." He was so right. Such a simple thing . . . to love God, to love yourself, to love your neighbor, to love those who hate you and give your life for others. It's so simple. And all the time those false disciples think they do.

"Beware of false prophets who come to you disguised as sheep but underneath are ravenous wolves. You will be able to tell them by their fruits." That is how the true disciple is recognized: He does

God's will.

Jesus told them what would happen to someone who didn't do God's will and built a house on sand, " . . . his teaching made a deep impression on the people because he taught them with authority, and not like their own scribes" (7, 28-29). Interesting. He taught them with authority. But today many won't accept his authority even as they didn't then.

Christ came to preach the kingdom of God to the poor. But they were so slow, like we are so slow to understand. They needed proof. So he proceeded to perform miracles.

I wish I could teach little children and older children today about the will of God. But how can I? It's a pre-evangelization period, so they tell me. There's loads of parents who don't know how to teach about God because they don't know him themselves. How can you teach what you don't know? Personally, Lord, if you ask me, I would simply say to all the parents, "Sit down, read the Bible, then go to some holy man or woman, and ask him or her to explain to you whatever you don't understand. Then you can teach your children."

When you are very poor it's easy to teach your child about God. And then when he HAS to go to a school that has catechism, He is the only Friend that the child and you have left. And the child understands it very quickly.

Miracles

What amuses me most, as well as amazes me most, in America and in Canada, is that people are astonished when a miracle takes place.

"Lord, why have You made them this way? It's like they have to see everything on TV, or hear about it on the radio, or touch everything to believe. And even then, half the time they don't believe."

Now we come to the cure of a leper.

After he had come down from the mountain, large crowds followed him. A leper now came up and bowed low in front of him, 'Sir,' he said, 'if you want to, you can cure me.' Jesus stretched out his hand and said, 'Of course I want to.' And his leprosy was cured at once. Then Jesus said to him, 'Mind you do not tell anyone, but go and show yourself to the priest and make the offering prescribed by Moses, as evidence for them' (8, 1-4).

I don't know enough about Mosaic customs, but I imagine you had to go and show yourself to the priest and make an offering.

One day I asked myself, "How much leprosy have you acquired, Catherine, all through your years?" I thought about the lecture bureau I was connected with and all the manipulations that went on in that business. Then I thought of the real estate deal I had been part of. The real estate people were selling half of Long Island. Fortunately, I only made one sale. One day a longtime resident of the area asked me, "Miss, were you the one who sold that property to those people? I wouldn't think with an honest face like yours that you would be party to such a rip-off." (In those days the word "rip-off" was not known but he used similar terms.) I was very surprised. "You can't put in any foundation because underneath is all sea water. This company you are with are all thieves and robbers, etc."

So I went to the police. They investigated and they said, yes, it was true. So I paid the buyer back. It took me a long time to pay back his down payment.

With these and similar incidents I remembered,

I came to think of myself as a pretty leprous person. True, I had confessed all my sins, such as they were. But somehow or other something lingered on. I asked myself, "Did you go and show yourself to the priest?" I decided I should go to the bishop of the diocese of Brooklyn where I lived.

Eventually I knocked at the door. It was quite an encounter. I said to him in my direct way, "I want to show myself to Your Excellency." I told him the story and added, "The Gospel says to go and show yourself to the priest. Here I am! If you want to ask me any questions, you are perfectly free to do so."

That poor Bishop didn't know what to do. He said, "I don't know exactly what you are talking about." I had read this passage so I quoted it, "The cure of a leper in Matthew," I said. He answered, "The cure of a leper in Matthew. Yes, yes, I know about that." I said, "Well, you know Jesus said, 'Go and show yourself . . . ' I figure out that you are the supreme priest." "But," he said, "have you been to confession." So I explained to him how my father had taught me to go to the Bishop when troubled in conscience. So he said, "Kneel down and I'll absolve you." But I'll tell you something. Every time he met me after that he would say, "I know, the leper woman." He didn't talk to me. I must have been a very crazy person when I was young.

Matthew goes on to the cure of the centurion's servant.

> When he went into Capernaum a centurion came up and pleaded with him. 'Sir,' he said, 'my servant is lying at home paralysed, and in great pain.' 'I will come myself and cure him,' said Jesus. The centurion replied, 'Sir, I am not worthy to have you under my roof; just give the word and my servant will be cured.

For I am under authority myself, and have soldiers under me; and I say to one man: Go, and he goes: to another: Come here, and he comes; to my servant: Do this, and he does it.' When Jesus heard this he was astonished and said to those following him, 'I tell you solemnly, nowhere in Israel have I found faith like this (8, 5-10).

Now there is the whole situation. It's faith that cures. The centurion believed. Do we? I can testify before God that, for fifty years, whatever I dreamt in the Lord has always come true for the Apostolate. So I am able to talk much about this, for as poor as I am even today, he hands me treasures all the time. Like the two or three houses that we opened in 1978. I just have to wish and he answers my prayer.

But strangely enough, all through my life, I haven't asked much for myself. I ask him to cure my knees if that be his will, but I'm perfectly willing not to be cured. I ask for myself the cure of my knees so that I can serve him better. But maybe bad knees serve him better than good knees.

I understand the importance of faith. Yes, indeed! He will not only cure the centurion's servant, he will build many communities for you . . . he will build apostolates . . . he will do many things . . . but you have to believe!

Yes, you have to believe, and that's the hardest thing in the world to do it seems. I don't know. I would not know how hard it is because when I was baptized on the day I was born in Nijni-Novgorod in a Pullman car on a train, I must have acquired from him the gift of faith, faith, faith. Because whatever happened to me, and a lot of things happened to me, faith sustained me through all my life. There were moments when it trembled, and yet it didn't. It was strong because I was so weak.

I love Jesus Christ, and when you love, you believe, you trust. There are no barriers between you and him whom you love. I trusted Eddie and Eddie trusted me. It's a funny thing, isn't it? Faith. I cannot explain it. All I know is that it is dark. Sometimes it is a stygian darkness. It's darker than midnight on the darkest night of the year.

But somehow, when you go through these terribly dark periods, as poor women like myself do for many, many years (I would say that I have walked in dark faith since the age of fifteen), then suddenly you enter into the light, for a moment or two, or ten, or a day or a week. It's so bright . . . so bright you can't explain it.

At the same time there is no fear in entering the darkness of faith. There is fear in entering all kinds of darknesses but not the darkness of faith. Because at the end of this long tunnel there is the Lord waiting for you.

As I read my Gospel I said to myself, "There is a miracle between every line of the Bible." But people don't notice it. They pass it by without noticing. I am a poor person. But I can tell about many miracles, official and unofficial. But let's see what Matthew has to say.

Today it's the cure of Peter's mother-in-law.

And going into Peter's house Jesus found Peter's mother-in-law in bed with fever. He touched her hand and the fever left her, and she got up and began to wait on him (8, 14-15).

I like that miracle. Because it says that as soon as she got better "she waited on him." Now that's the way I feel — that I'm all ready to wait on him. All ready!

There are so many "miracles" happening now due to the Charismatic Renewal. But I want to ask those people if as soon as they are cured, do they "wait" on the Lord. For these days he needs to be "waited" upon more than ever.

> That evening they brought him many who were possessed by devils. He cast out the spirits with a word and cured all who were sick. This was to fulfil the prophecy of Isaiah: He took our sicknesses away and carried our diseases for us (8, 16-17).

That is true. And he asks the same of us who want to follow him, especially the poor.

"Lord, I have never understood it. I guess I'll never understand. I suppose that's the darkness of faith I have to go through. But it seems as if you select specifically some people. You take the sickness of the world, the diseases of the world, and you put it all on the back of the poor. Why? Why is it that so many poor have to carry the diseases and the sicknesses of the world? Why you do that I wish I knew."

It's getting dark in my room. It's a hot and humid day.

"Suddenly it's as if I were walking through a long corridor, Lord, for I am poor too. Poorer perhaps than any other poor that you've met. And it seems as if you have put the burden of many people on my shoulders. The corridor is so long, so dark, that I lose all understanding. And perhaps that is the greatest poverty of all: not understanding. But while I am walking this corridor I understand one thing, Lord. True, all this is put on my shoulders. True, I can feel it. But at the same time *you put faith* into my heart. And so it seems that in my dark room, with the sea battering the shores of my utter incomprehension, you are putting me to the test. You are testing my Faith.

"Well, if that be it, Lord, here, you have it. Whatever faith is needed, I give to you. A poor woman's faith is not much, and yet I know it is, especially because she is poor. She followed you. That's how she became poor." Yes, a poor woman's faith might really save the world.

Strange how a lot of ideas come into my head.

> When Jesus saw the great crowds all about him he gave orders to leave for the other side. One of the scribes then came up and said to him, 'Master, I will follow you wherever you go.' Jesus replied, 'Foxes have holes and the birds of the air have nests, but the Son of Man has nowhere to lay his head.'

> Another man, one of his disciples, said to him, 'Sir, let me go and bury my father first.' But Jesus replied, 'Follow me, and leave the dead to bury their dead' (8, 18-22).

This paragraph of Matthew's Gospel is entitled "Hardships of the Apostolic Calling." There is no denying that there are a lot of hardships in the apostolic calling!

"Sometimes, my friend, my beloved Jesus Christ, you can make me laugh. There is nothing harder than the apostolic calling and you know it! You know it very well. It is good that you put the idea in St. Matthew's head. Personally I would like more on the subject, say a hundred pages or so. But you let me sit here in my little room and figure it out for myself. Well, I can figure it out for myself.

"I know, for instance, that all Christians are apostles. You made *all* Christians apostles. You told them to go and preach the word. That is to say, the Gospel . . . your Gospel. And you warned them! You warned them that they would be called before the Sanhedrin and perhaps be killed. You remember what Dostoevsky wrote about the Grand Inquisitor. And then there are all your martyrs, all your confessors.

What a long line.

"But I feel so sorry for you. I'd like to cradle you in my arms and kiss your tears away. I don't know why it seems to me that you are crying. You know why? Because we needn't have that poverty. We needn't have any of those things, if we only obeyed your commandments. Yes, that's the way it is. Maybe you could kiss my tears away, and I yours. We're both kind of lonely people, you and I."

But Matthew goes on:

> Then he got into the boat followed by his disciples. Without warning a storm broke over the lake, so violent that the waves were breaking right over the boat. But he was asleep. So they went to him and woke him saying, 'Save us, Lord, we are going down!' And he said to them, 'Why are you so frightened, you men of little faith?' And with that he stood up and rebuked the winds and the sea; and all was calm again. The men were astounded and said, 'What kind of man is this? Even the winds and the sea obey him' (8, 23-27).

Here I am standing by the sea, let us say. Suppose I really believe and I say "Stop" to the heavy waves. "Stop. I want to get some more shells. And wind, blow a fresh breeze through the whole island until I leave . . . blow, blow, blow! Sun! Stay home . . . don't get up!" Do you think God would answer my prayer? I don't think so. You know why? Because it will benefit no one; there is nobody to save. You don't do miracles just for fun.

"The Apostles thought they were going to perish. They didn't know who you were and you saved them. If we were in a boat out on the sea, you would save us too.

"But shells are little things. We can play with shells, you and I. Well, I'll leave it to you. Shells are the playthings of the poor, just like marbles or stones easily come by. You might change your mind and give me a cool wind, no sun, and a quiet sea. Although it's stupid to ask for that, because if I ask for the wind, then the sea will be rough. Oh, well, that's just a conversation with you, Lord. You know how I talk with you always."

When he reached the country of the Gadarnes on the other side, two demonaics came towards him out of the tombs — creatures so fierce that nobody could pass that way. They stood there shouting, 'What do you want with us, Son of God? Have you come here to torture us before the time?' Now some distance away there was a large herd of pigs feeding, and the devils pleaded with Jesus, 'If you cast us out, send us into the herd of pigs.' And he said to them, 'Go then,' and they came out and made for the pigs; and at that the whole herd charged down the cliff into the lake and perished in the water. The swineherds ran off and made for the town, where they told the whole story, including what had happened to the demonaics. At this the whole town set out to meet Jesus; and as soon as they saw him they implored him to leave the neighborhood (8, 28-34).

There are miracles and miracles! "Lord, you know why you had to leave the neighborhood? Because it was a whole herd of swine and there was a big loss of money. People like you are not tolerated."

"I understand that, Lord. It's very simple. You come to a big city. You have no job. You go to the place where your cross shines on the roof, and they throw you out! You go to another place which shouts in neon lights, 'Jesus Saves!', and they barely accept you. People who follow you have really nowhere to lay their head. Nowhere at all.

"He got back in the boat," Matthew continues, "crossed the water and came to his own town. Then

some people appeared, bringing him a paralytic
stretched out on a bed. Seeing their faith Jesus said to
the paralytic, 'Courage, my child, your sins are
forgiven'" (9, 1-2).

"Lord, do I believe or don't I believe? My knees
could be cured but I can't ask for that because it seems
that you have given to me (who was so fleet of foot)
this lameness specifically as a sign of my poverty, so I
should never forget it. Isaiah said, 'And yet ours were
the sufferings he bore, ours the sorrows he carried'
(53,4). Perhaps that is what you want me to do.
Because it has added to my poverty. I ask you to cure
it, but you know and I know that it's not too exciting.
I mean, I'm not spending nights praying to you for a
cure. Just occasionally. If you want to, okay, but I
think there is something in my lameness that you
want. And you can have it. I don't think it cures lame
people across the world. I think that you use it to cure
lame souls. You're welcome to it."

EIGHT

MATTHEW'S OWN CALL

Now we come to Matthew's own call. "As Jesus was walking on from there he saw a man named Matthew sitting by the customs house, and he said to him, 'Follow me.' And he got up and followed him" (9, 9-10).

Ever think of that? I saw a painting, the work of a great artist, somewhere, someplace in Europe, in which Jesus is walking, his head is slightly turned, and Matthew has overturned his tax collector's table, and all the money is on the ground. Some kids are collecting the money. Matthew doesn't look at them. He follows Christ.

How I wish I were like that. That's why I must study the Gospel from his point of view. So many things occur in one's life that show you how poor you are. And I thank God. "Really, I thank you, Lord, for letting me know quite a while ago how poor I was. And also that I had to be as open to **you** as an empty shell, for **you** wanted to put the gold of your words in me. Thank you!"

While he was at dinner in the house it happened that a number of tax collectors and sinners came to sit at the table with Jesus and his disciples. When the Pharisees saw this, they said to his disciples, 'Why does your master eat with tax collectors and sinners?' When he heard this he replied, 'It is not the healthy who need the doctor, but the sick. Go and learn the meaning of the words: What I want is mercy, not sacrifice. And indeed I did not come to call the virtuous, but sinners' (9, 10-13).

There was Matthew, and he had followed Christ immediately! Without thinking. That's what I call a vocation. Naturally, all the tax collectors came around probably to wish him well or to find out who this man was that he followed. Obviously! And what could Jesus do but eat with them? They were pleasant people. Was it their fault they had to collect taxes? No. So there they were having a nice time as only Jesus could make it. I bet you a supper with Jesus was wonderful! Even if there was only plain bread to eat.

There they were having a good time and who should come around? Pharisees, Sadducees. I think they were spoil sports! Long faces!! They'd make any child think of castor oil. They make ME think of castor oil, and I'm no child! So Jesus Christ told them that he was a physician, and that he came for the sick. "What I want is mercy, not sacrifice." That's what his Father said, long ago and far away in the Old Testament. But those characters who were supposed to explain the Old Testament to the people didn't care about *his* explanation a bit!

Why Are the Labourers Few?

Jesus made a tour through all the towns and villages, teaching in their synagogues, proclaiming the Good News of the kingdom and curing all kinds of diseases and sickness.

And when he saw the crowds he felt sorry for them because they were harassed and dejected, like sheep without a shepherd. Then he said to his disciples, 'The harvest is rich but the labourers are few, so ask the Lord of the harvest to send labourers to his harvest' (9, 32-37).

THAT is what interests me. He made a tour. And so should we. We should be pilgrims.

Why is the harvest rich but the labourers few? Yes, that is what I thought about yesterday and the day before, and twenty years ago, and even when I was a little girl. I asked some nun if God wanted labourers why didn't he make them? When I was little I thought that God could make everything! But here is what Matthew says as he discusses the instructions of Christ:

> He summoned his twelve disciples, and gave them authority over unclean spirits with power to cast them out and to cure all kinds of diseases and sickness (10,1).

What an immense power the priests have, and the bishops! But they don't use it very much. They haven't used it very much. In that sense the Charismatic Renewal is a very good thing. The only reason that I feel sad about it is that it isn't integrated enough into the parish. Alas, the trouble is that the parish is not the center of the Christian life at this present moment. Everything else is. I meditate a lot on those pages of this Gospel of mine.

The Incarnation allowed God to preach as he did. Now, because of his Incarnation, we are incarnated in him, that it is time for us to preach like he did. Simple, plain language, parables that fishermen and agricultural workers, scientists and students and everybody in-between can understand. We have to learn, to re-learn the way to the human heart.

Human speech is the echo of God's voice. Speech has been given to us by God so that we might preach his Gospel to one another and also that we might talk to him. Alas, very few people these days talk to God or about God, though more and more do.

"He summoned the twelve disciples and gave them authority . . . ." I think of the tremendous authority he gave them. That's what I wrote in *Dear*

Father. That book speaks of a mystery I approach in fear and trembling . " . . . and gave them authority over unclean spirits with power to cast them out and to cure all kinds of diseases and sickness."

Why have we forgotten this? It is because we have been separated from the Church. Secularism and its reliance on new ideas and technology have drawn us away from God. But we're slowly coming back, for the Spirit is still alive amongst us.

> Whatever town or village you go into, ask for someone trustworthy and stay with him until you leave. As you enter his house, salute it, and if the house deserves it, let your peace descend upon it; if it does not, let your peace come back to you. And if anyone does not welcome you or listen to what you have to say, as you walk out of the house or town shake the dust from your feet. I tell you solemnly, on the day of Judgement it will not go as hard with the land of Sodom and Gomorrah as with that town. Remember, I am sending you out like sheep among wolves; so be cunning as serpents and yet as harmless as doves (10, 11-16).

Yes, as cunning as serpents and as harmless as doves. Nobody these days wants to be that. It is as if the cursed tree, with the little brown apples that were in the garden of Eden . . . the symbolic tree . . . continues to poison everybody. The manchineel tree is poisonous, but it has beautiful little apples. It is also attractive. But even if you cut a branch off and touch the juice you will find that it is a very dangerous tree. It burns the skin. And if you swallow the apples you die.

Well, I think that the manchineel is the transplanted Tree of Good and Evil. Surely when you eat of it, or touch it or whatever, you certainly will know evil, though the apples are so attractive. It seems to me that we are still tempted with the same old thing. Here I am in great poverty, having nothing. I can truthfully say that my dead hands will take nothing with them. Just a silver cross will be on my breast. It has been given to me. I didn't make it. Yes, I won't have anything, so all will be well.

I have given everything to God, seemingly, so far. There is one thing left, our Apostolate, the one he created through me. If he wants it, I surrender it gladly. It's nice to be very poor. It's nice to be so very poor that you can always give God atonement. No matter how poor I am, I can atone for myself and others.

"Do not turn your steps to pagan territory . . . " (10,6). Now I'm not quite clear why he wouldn't let them go to the Gentiles, but probably it was not the time. He sent them to the house of Israel.

But he himself went into the Samaritan town with this woman who was at the well. At first, he didn't enter the town, but she brought the town to him. It's a little bit incomprehensible, but then Christ always is a little bit incomprehensible, right?

NINE

RISK

It came to me late one evening that the many things written in the Gospel are all true, but that I hadn't really faced myself. I realized that even though I had read the Gospels (you might say without stopping) through my whole life, even though my Book's pages were all curled up, I again wondered to myself: why is it that people don't accept the Gospel?

That evening I understood why. It's because the Gospel, in fact, the whole of the Bible, is calling man to a RISK.

Christ does not preach "liberation theology," nor is he a German philosopher. Not at all. But he asks for risk, and that is why people don't want to follow him. That's why they stay away. Yet they want to make believe that they're Christian. I realize that myself. Don't you realize that within yourself? When you stop to think about it, do *you* want to risk your whole life on the word of a man?

"No," I said to myself, "No. It's too risky." That is the real reason why people don't want to follow the Gospel. It demands too much.

> Anyone who prefers father or mother to me is not worthy of me. Anyone who prefers son or daughter to me is not worthy of me. Anyone who does not take his cross and follow in my footsteps is not worthy of me. Anyone who finds his life will lose it; anyone who loses his life for my sake will find it (10, 37-39).

Now, what kind of speech is that, I ask you? I sat there in my room. It was a balmy evening and I had my window open. The muted noises of the city came wafting in, but they seemed to disappear as I contemplated these fantastic ideas of Jesus Christ.

No wonder nobody wants to follow him, "Anyone who prefers father or mother to me is not worthy of me." Why not? "Anyone who prefers sons or daughters to me is not worthy of me." Give it a thought! Give it a thought! You are a woman; you give birth. You hold that little infant in your arms, girl or boy. You see it grow up and bingo! you have to let it go. You can't prefer it to Jesus Christ. And then, "Anyone who does not take his cross and follow in my footsteps is not worthy of me." Get the picture? A cross is a heavy thing.

On top of this, he says he has come "to set a man against his father, a daughter against her mother, a daughter-in-law against her mother-in-law. A man's enemies will be those of his own household" (11,35). So then, he says that you have to give up your father and mother and brothers, sisters, everybody!

Sitting by an open window, I hardly heard the noises of the city, for I was in deep thought: the reason we don't follow Christ is because of *risk*. There is no way of escaping that fact. The Gospels are like a mirror revealing me to myself. There is no one in the room at all. There is only darkness, an open window, noises from the city, and a mirror which accuses me. Why do I shiver on this warm June night?

What am I talking about? I'm talking about the heart of what Jesus Christ is and said. As I write these words, a lot of philosophers and theologians discuss a lot of things: "Is Christ God? Is he the Son of God? Did he rise from the dead?" How sad! The point is that those nice gentlemen, whoever they are, plus millions of others who are supposed to be Christian, ARE NOT

TAKING THE RISK of following Christ. It's all very well to read and write, but it's the *doing* that is difficult.

Now take me. A poor woman has to take risks all day long. Going to work from home these days is risky. And coming back at night. Everytime I open my mouth I take a risk. What do I risk? I risk the disapproval of people, the anger of people, the dislike of people.

There is a town called Timmins in Canada. I was invited to lecture there about Russia. It was in the very early days of my arrival in Canada. I was describing the Communist Revolution, and what it did to my family, when zip! A knife whizzed by me. A "Pukko" as it is called in Finnish. Followed by another "Pukko."

A constable of the Royal Canadian Mounted Police jumped up in the audience, rushed to the stage, got his revolver out and sat by me. I looked at the Pukkos and I looked at the audience that was somewhat stunned, and I continued to lecture. The audience applauded. I spoke about Christ and atheism, of the struggle between good and evil. There is your problem. I opened my mouth and I got pukkos. In other words, I was taking a big risk.

Similar things happened to me in the south at the hands of the Ku Klux Klan, and in other circumstances.

Christ warned us: whenever you preach you take a risk. That's nothing new. "Beware of men: they will hand you over to sanhedrins and scourge you in their synagogues" (10,17). That's what will happen to you, make no mistake about it.

So it's very risky to follow Christ, and that's why few do! Dear reader, think about that yourself, because each one has to face a different risk!

Now we come to the mystery of the kingdom of

heaven. I say that's the same risk. I mean anybody who puts a foot into the beginning of the mystery is risking his life. Otherwise he is doing what Christ asked him to do. " . . . anyone who loses his life for my sake will find it" (11,39).

"When Jesus had finished instructing his twelve disciples he moved on from there to teach and preach in their towns. Now John in his prison had heard what Christ was doing and he sent his disciples to ask him, 'Are you the one who is to come, or have we got to wait for someone else?'" (11, 1-3) John sent his disciples to Jesus so that they might be convinced. Maybe I should do the same thing with the members of Madonna House — send them to Jesus with their questions. It would be a good idea.

> 'Are you the one who is to come, or have we got to
> wait for someone else?' Jesus answered, 'Go back and
> tell John what you hear and see; the blind see again,
> and the lame walk, lepers are cleansed, and the deaf
> hear, and the dead are raised to life, and the Good
> News is proclaimed to the poor; and happy is the man
> who does not lose faith in me' (11, 3-5).

Now that is superb stuff! Here is your risk. "Happy is the man who does not lose faith in me" (11,5). That's what we haven't got today. I mean, honestly . . . that makes me feel sad. "Happy is the man who does not lose faith in me." But all around me and all about me men are losing faith in him all the time. And as far as I am concerned, we who should know all about him present him very poorly. We just don't preach that the following of Christ is a risk. We put lots of jam on top of the truth and we say, "Well, you can eat that." That's wrong. When you deal with Christ you must feed people bread and wine, and nothing else. Don't sweeten Christ's teaching.

When you deal with Christ you never look back. Always forward. He is walking on the water. And if he calls me, I will have to go and walk on the water. Always following him. Always your heart moving toward him, without counting the cost. That's an absolute necessity. If you're going to count the cost of following Christ, you might as well stay at home. Nobody ought to keep a record of what it costs to follow Christ. That's idiotic.

The Gospel I was reading continues: "What description can I find for this generation? It is like children shouting to each other as they sit in the market place: 'We played the pipes for you, and you wouldn't dance; we sang dirges, and you wouldn't be mourners.' For John came, neither eating nor drinking, and they say, 'He is possessed.' The Son of Man came, eating and drinking, and they say, 'Look, a glutton and a drunkard, a friend of tax collectors and sinners.' Yet wisdom has been proved right by her actions" (11, 16-19).

Well, it's so clear that even I, a poor woman with not too much education in Scripture, can understand. It's so simple. John was the messenger whom God the Father sent ahead of Jesus Christ to prepare his way, to straighten out his way, to flatten out the rocks and level mountains. But don't make a mistake. He's constantly sending people ahead of himself to proclaim the coming of his kingdom.

Most of us spend our time trying to obliterate the path of the Lord. Each Catholic, and all of us, must constantly *restore* the path of the Lord. To restore the path of the Lord is a slow business, and yet a constant business, a daily business made up of little things which overcome evil.

When faced with the devil, if you REALLY

believe in Christ, all you have to do is say a little prayer, make the Sign of the Cross, and say, "Lord, where is that path that St. John the Baptist started?" And bingo! It appears right in front of you. You don't care if it hurts or not. You don't care if you leave bloody footprints, because as you walk it becomes smooth. And it's a new path for someone else to follow. If you keep on walking, your feet don't get tired. They don't hurt. What was bloody today is not bloody tomorrow. And you make a new road for the Lord. Yes, even a poor woman with little education can understand that. That each one of us has to make a path, has to restore the path of St. John, is obvious.

Then he began to reproach them. And it's high time he did! He began to reproach the towns in which most of his miracles had been worked, because they refused to repent.

> Alas for you, Chorazin! Alas for you, Bethsaida! For if the miracles done in you had been done in Tyre and Sidon, they would have repented long ago in sackcloth and ashes. And still, I tell you that it will not go as hard on Judgement day with Tyre and Sidon as with you. And as for you, Capernaum, did you want to be exalted as high as heaven? You shall be thrown down to hell. For if the miracles done in you had been done in Sidon, it would have been standing yet. And still, I tell you that it will not go as hard with the land of Sodom on Judgement day as with you (11, 20-24).

What I understand, and what poor people understand, is that you cannot constantly throw the gauntlet in the face of God. Oh, Jesus will always turn his cheek so that you can hit him. But what about his Father? How long do you think his Father is going to stand the ill treatment of his Son? Not long.

I think that the age of the catacombs and the desert is at hand.

Good News

Factually, when you're in love with God as I have been all my life, there is only one book you can read: *The Gospel.* Oh, the whole Bible is extraordinary, but the Gospel is the real one for me. I find that you're never lonely when you read the Gospel. Though, to be frank, I experienced loneliness of a sort all of my life. There was Eddie, of course, my second husband. I was very happy with him, but that didn't last. It's strange. God always seemed to give me things and then take them away. I often wondered about that. True, he said that you have to give everything up for him. But it sort of happened without you really knowing about it.

Now there are thousands of women like myself, millions! They are not versed in the Scriptures, but they derive a tremendous strength from it. "As long as you can read," said the pilgrim of the *Way of a Pilgrim,* "the Gospel is your consolation." That's true. That's absolutely true as far as I'm concerned. The Gospel is my consolation. But it is far more than that. These days everybody wants to ask me a whole series of questions. "Who are you? Where do you come from, etc.?" That seems so funny to me because you don't find out anything about people by asking questions. (Unless, of course, it's a criminal investigation!) If you started to ask me questions, you would get nowhere.

Eddie did that when he wrote *Tumbleweed.* He started asking me questions. Because I was half in love with him, I answered his questions. But when the book came out, the questions kind of got lost in a love affair between two people. So you really can be lonely when you haven't got the book, the Old and New Testament.

At that time Jesus exclaimed, 'I bless you, Father, Lord of heaven and of earth, for hiding these things from the learned and the clever and revealing them to mere children. Yes, Father, for that is what it pleased you to do. Everything has been entrusted to me by my Father; and no one knows the Son except the Father, just as no one knows the Father except the Son and those to whom the Son chooses to reveal him' (11, 25-27).

Now I like that very much. I really do. Because it talks about me. God himself says it. It makes you feel very good. At least it makes me feel very good for I'm a poor woman.

Come to me, all you who labour and are overburdened, and I will give you rest. Shoulder my yoke and learn from me, for I am gentle and humble in heart, and you will find rest for your souls. Yes, my yoke is easy and my burden light (11, 28-30).

Well, that's a new translation. I mislaid somewhere my old Gospel. This is from a new Gospel. It's not as good as the old one but it too reveals the gentleness of Christ.

Lay your burdens down! That's what I'm trying to tell my community. But they don't understand. It's so very simple. First, if you are thirsty, go to him. That's number one. Bread and wine will satisfy you and then you will find rest for your soul.

North Americans are on a train that just won't stop . . . choo, choo, choo . . . always going, never stopping. But lately the desert through which the train passes is dotted with poustinias. There are little houses where they can rest. And they do.

I like that, "Come to me all you who labour and are overburdened." I can see a thousand, a million people . . . poor people. Sure, I said, this is a poor *woman's* Gospel, but it's also a poor *man's* Gospel. Man, woman, they come to Jesus to do just that: rest.

His yoke is easy and his burden is light, provided that
you believe in him. You need faith. That's another
thing people lack these days. You have to pray about
that very much.

> At that time Jesus took a walk one sabbath through
> the cornfields. His disciples were hungry and began to
> pick ears of corn and eat them. The Pharisees noticed
> it and said to him, 'Look, your disciples are doing
> something that is forbidden on the sabbath' (12, 1-2).

When I think of the poor people, men and women,
myself included, the sabbath rest does not apply to us.
We so often have to do servile work on Sunday.
Suppose you're a waitress earning your living. You're
going to work eight hours even on Sunday because
people have to eat. In fact, there are other works you
have to do when you're poor.

Sunday, our sabbath, seems to have lost much of
its sanctity. I think it has lost its power or holiness
because it has not been revered by those who were the
teachers of the sabbath. I remember when I was in the
Holy Land, many Jews went someplace else on the
sabbath, where they did not have to observe it. I
wonder how many VIPs observe the sabbath in Israel.

I feel very sad these days. In every city I see a big,
big excavation. Everywhere — in New York, Paris,
Berlin, London and many other places — men have
dug immense holes. People throw in them all the
beautiful things that once meant so much to life: the
family, the Sabbath, even Christ's Resurrection.
Throw it in! We don't believe in that! Actually, we
don't believe in very much. So how can we ask people
to say Credo when there is that huge hole in every town
into which we throw most of our truths?

I have never felt so poor as I feel in Madonna

House these days. When I landed in the Bowery begging food from a "Jesus Saves" mission, and a Jewish taxi driver took me to his home and fed me, I felt rich compared to what I feel now. Today I'm really poor. It's not because I'm completely ready to give up the Apostolate; that is not poverty. God gives me a gift and I return it to him. He wants to detach me, and attach me to himself. That's no problem.

My poverty shines like a burnished icon in the hearts of my spiritual children. There is something I haven't done. Something I haven't finished. Something I haven't conveyed. All around me I see all those things I haven't conveyed, and my poverty is so excessive. I seem to be covered with rags. I seem to have nowhere to lay my head. I seem to be lost in some sort of fog. I know that I'm a woman who is poor. I know next to me stand thousands like me. But not everyone is a foundress of an **apostolate** of the Lord. And it is in the very essence of that apostolate that my poverty is mostly visible. There is something there that I have missed. I haven't done something. I haven't prayed enough. I don't know what it is. I really don't. But I feel heavily burdened.

The Gospel goes on.

> He moved on from there and went to their synagogue, and a man was there at the time who had a withered hand. They asked him, 'Is it against the law to cure a man on the sabbath day?' hoping for something to use against him. But he said to them, 'If any one of you here had only one sheep, and it fell down a hole on the sabbath day, would he not get hold of it and lift it out? Now a man is far more important than a sheep, so it follows that it is permitted to do good on the sabbath day.' Then he said to the man, 'Stretch out your hand.' He stretched it out and his hand was better, as sound as the other one. At this the Pharisees went out and began

to plot against him, discussing how to destroy him (12, 9-14).

Here you really have it. A poor woman like myself, and all of us who are poor together, have to watch every day the destruction, the plotting to destroy God. Some theologians, it seems, are plotting. The atheists are plotting. All kinds of people are plotting. Divisiveness is everywhere, and divisiveness breaks everything up. That's why the world is breaking up. The family is breaking up.

But Matthew goes on to say,

Jesus knew this . . . and withdrew from the district. Many followed him and he cured them all, but warned them not to make him known. This was to fulfill the prophecy of Isaiah:

Here is my servant whom I have chosen,
my beloved, the favourite of my soul.
I will endow him with my spirit,
and he will proclaim the true faith to the nations.
He will not brawl or shout,
nor will anyone hear his voice in the streets.
He will not break the crushed reed,
nor put out the smouldering wick
till he has led the truth to victory:
in his name the nations will put their hope.
(12, 15-21)

Well, it's very difficult for a poor person like myself to believe in this prophecy of Isaiah, except in darkness, because all around and about me what do I see? The opposite! Exactly the opposite. They shout and they proclaim and they want to make a pornographic movie about Christ.

It's difficult! Poor and rich alike these days have to pray and implore God for faith. That's our wealth and that's our poverty. Too many technological marvels happen. It seems as if we have succumbed to the devil's "temptations in the desert." It's difficult . . . but not impossible . . . to believe.

TEN

NOT WITHOUT PARABLES

Well, he spoke in parables, and it appeared that he didn't speak without parables. I know that he speaks in parables to all those who love him and who love the signs of God in nature and in everything that surrounds us. Yes, all of us who love nature speak in symbols and in parables. Always meaning something else. Take, for instance, the first Russian stories. They were transmitted orally. Eventually Pushkin and Joukoffsky wrote them down. They're called Belini. Those are the first oral stories. I use them on New Year's Eve. For instance: "It isn't the wheat that is bending low before the wind, it is the son who is bowing low before his father." He wants to ask permission to go and do whatever the story talks about.

Jesus being an Easterner spoke symbolically, for the Jews love symbols.

I was sitting there, thinking to myself, "That's all very well and fine. You even wrote a book called *Not Without Parables*. But now take your Bible, my dear. I know it's getting dirty and old, but no Bible ever gets dirty and no Bible ever gets old. Let's see how parables apply today."

> That same day, Jesus left the house and sat by the lakeside, but such crowds gathered around him that he got into a boat and sat there. The people all stood on the beach, and he told them many things in parables (13, 1-3).

Isn't that imaginative? But today, in the strange fortresses we call cities, all parables are vanishing.

They creep into basements, into all kinds of holes, and
they just disappear. The young ones hunger for
parables and they go aseeking. Where? To the Byzantine people, the Byzantine Rite, the Eastern Rite, the
Eastern religions, which have mysterious significance.
But all they have to do is take up the Bible. I have a
little Bible. I can read it. I don't have to go to India or
anywhere else for mystery and symbols. I find them on
every page of my Bible. I can find them myself. Here
is one.

> Imagine a sower going to sow. As he sowed, some of
> the seeds fell on the edge of the path, and the birds
> came and ate them up. Others fell on patches or rock
> where they found little soil and sprang up straight
> away, because there was no depth of earth; but as soon
> as the sun came up they were scorched and, not having
> any roots, they withered away. Others fell among
> thorns, and the thorns grew up and choked them.
> Others fell on rich soil and produced their crop, some a
> hundredfold, some sixty, some thirty. Listen, anyone
> who has ears! (13, 1-9)

Jesus Christ instructs you very simply. Stop.
Think awhile. Apply yourself. Life is not all mathe-
matical equations. We are not computers. There is
lots of fun in language, in parables, and in signs.

The Pharisees, though, were the big shots. People
thought they really amounted to something. But
factually, they were tin horns. They only knew law and
order. They didn't listen to Jesus. They never learned.

It doesn't take a Ph.D. to understand right away
what Jesus says here. It's obvious. It's as obvious as the
nose on your face. True, you need a mirror to see your
nose, but if you have faith you have a mirror.

You absorb God's words. They go deep into your
heart. And you understand, even if you are illiterate.

You peek into your heart and what do you see? It's not stony; there are no weeds for the words of God to fall into and die. No, it's a nicely cultivated land. And who cultivated it? You did! And how did you do it? Well, first and foremost, you realized what your baptism meant, and that it brought you right into the death and life of Jesus Christ. And obviously, that you were meant to be, therefore, a co-worker of his. He said, "He who is not with me is against me" (12,30). So, presumably, if you are really a believer, you are with him, and if you are with him, you do have a little seed pouch, and you sow from it. Your seeds do take root because you have made straight the paths of the Lord. Now does it take a Ph.D. to find that out? Not at all.

Then the disciples went up to him and asked, 'Why do you talk to them in parables?' 'Because,' he replied, 'the mysteries of the kingdom of heaven are revealed to you, but they are not revealed to them. For anyone who has will be given more, and he will have more than enough; but from anyone who has not, even what he has will be taken away. The reason I talk to them in parables is that they look without seeing and listen without hearing or understanding. So in their case this prophecy of Isaiah is being fulfilled:

You will listen and listen again, but not
    understand,
see and see again, but not perceive.
For the heart of this nation has grown coarse,
their ears are dull of hearing, and they have
    shut their eyes,
for fear they should see with their eyes,
hear with their ears,
understand with their heart,
and be converted
and be healed by me.

'But happy are your eyes because they see, your ears

because they hear! I tell you solemnly, many prophets
and holy men longed to see what you see, and never
saw it; to hear what you hear, and never heard it'
(13, 10-17).

This is superb! Jesus tells them exactly what's
what. If he came to supper today he would do the same.
Or would he? "You have ears and do not hear. You
have eyes and do not see." This is the tragedy of the
New World — I don't know about the other countries
— but really they don't see and they don't hear. It
seems that we do not concentrate. Sometimes I notice
people when priests speak to them or some important
lecturer. They seem to be distracted. For instance, one
girl is so nervous she moves her feet all the time. So she
can't hear. Another yawns. A third one sleeps. A few
listen. That's the sadness that comes into my heart.
They really don't hear.

The only thing I pray to God is that he forgive
them because if they can't hear his voice, they cannot
live the Gospel without compromise. It's very important to understand that.

When I was very poor these parables sustained
me. They sustained me because I was close to nature
and close to people. One can be close to nature in the
midst of city slums and city streets, for symbols are
not only found in forests and fields but all around you.

Take 42nd Street and Broadway with its unending
traffic of people and vehicles. I used to stand there and
experience the solitude of the poustinia.

More than streets, more than symbols of things,
there are symbols in people. In them I saw beautiful
things.

There are incidents in my life which I shall always
remember: the Jewish taxi driver, for instance. He's
probably in heaven now, but I pray for his family every

day. He understood much and revealed much to me of the goodness of God. And so did many others: prostitutes and priests, old women and young. They stand out as signs and parables in my life.

I lectured in St. Louis in a Unitarian Church. I shall never forget it, because after the lecture the minister took me to his house and confessed that he was a priest. He fell on his knees, put his face into my lap, and cried and cried and cried. He had a wife. This was long ago, long before Vatican II. The Bishop sent him to the Trappists. He had written on the Trinity and gotten all mixed up about it, married his nurse and joined the Unitarians. I thought of the parable of the Prodigal Son and for a moment I felt like a Father.

I was still a poor woman. I still hadn't studied. I still didn't have a Ph.D. in Scripture but I had words that were symbolic and moved human beings. They came to me from my Eastern heritage.

So those are happy who see and hear. He explains the parable of the sower. But I don't understand why he should. To me the parable of the sower doesn't need any explanation. But he explained it to his disciples. That's what I couldn't understand.

I feel that the parables are a prolongation of the eternal richness of God. I have a slightly childish idea about them. It seems to me that God puts toys in between the words for us poor women and children and men to find. They are toys for children but also food for men and women. The wealth of the Gospel is ours. The Gospel is preached to the poor. And are we not all poor? Yes, I love the Gospels!

Everything, **every time** is new. I just opened my Bible and my eyes fell on these words: "My eyes yearn to see your promise. When will you console me?" (Ps 121,1) You see that the Old Testament flows into the New and the New Testament reveals its secrets. The simpler you are, the humbler you are, the quicker are the secrets revealed. You really don't have to agonize over the parables. It's reality. When I say, "It's not wheat bowing its head under the wind, it is a son bowing before his father," I'm clear. I don't need anybody to explain it to me. Because I'm Russian, this thing is clear to me. The same way when I read the Gospel, it's clear to me. The Gospel exists to help people like me. I don't need explanations because I have listened, and because he who is the Gospel clarified it for me. After all, there is no better Teacher than God.

Well, I must admit that here is the parable of the darnel. Now what is a darnel? Well, read and find out, as the saying goes. It's worth reading and thinking about.

God is always approached in a friendly fashion and respectfully. Maybe he doesn't want to give you a parable. Maybe he just wants to talk to you.

> He put another parable before them: 'The kingdom of heaven may be compared to a man who sowed good seed in his field. While everybody was asleep his enemy came, sowed darnel all among the wheat, and made off. When the new wheat sprouted and ripened, the darnel appeared as well. The owner's servants went to him and said, "Sir, was it not good seed that you sowed in your field? If so, where does the darnel come from?" "Some enemy has done this," he answered. And the servants said, "Do you want us to go and weed it out?" But he said, "No, because when you weed out the darnel you might pull up the wheat with it. Let them both grow till the harvest; and at harvest time I shall say to the reapers: First collect the darnel and tie it in bundles to be burnt, then gather the wheat into my barn"'   (13, 24-30).

That's quite something to think about. I remember, as a member of the Third Order to which I belonged, I was visiting an old lady in Chicago. She was very old, in her eighties, all crippled with arthritis, and I used to do her shopping for her. She constantly bemoaned the sinfulness of her youth. I got a little tired of that and picked up my Gospel, the one with the pages all curled up. I found Matthew and I read to her this parable.

I said to her, "So maybe you were a bad weed in your youth, and that was too bad. But there's one consolation you have in being darnel: you grew side by side with wheat. So all you have to do now is pray to God to change you into wheat." We talked about it again and again and again. She said, "Do you think it's too late for me to be changed into wheat?" I said, "Not at all."

I knelt down by her bed and together we recited the following prayers: (she did mostly), "Lord, I didn't even know what darnel was, and, to be absolutely truthful, I still don't. But in your book you say it is a bad thing. That was me. I was darnel when I was young. It reminds me of the darning needles. That's what I associated the word with. But then I'm old and uneducated. You know what I used to do, Lord? I used to sneak out when my mother was away and I had fun with the boys. My mother always found out because my darning was always so bad. This lady says that darnel is something else. But you have given me length of days to grow with the wheat." Then she turned around to me, "Katie, suppose that you start praying. I've done my praying." So I turned around to God and I said, "She wants to be a grain of wheat, just a little grain of wheat, that's all." Of course, the Lord had no problem with that. He just smiled, lifted his head, and she was changed into wheat.

She said to me, "Look, Katie, I really feel different. Right now I feel good. I'm wheat." And she was telling everybody that she was wheat. Some people thought she was crazy.

> Here is another picture of the kingdom of heaven.
> 'Again, the kingdom of heaven is like a merchant looking for fine pearls; when he finds one of great value he goes and sells everything he owns and buys it.
>
> 'Again, the kingdom of heaven is like a dragnet cast into the sea that brings in a haul of all kinds. When it is full, the fishermen haul it ashore; then, sitting down, they collect the good ones in a basket and throw away those that are no use. That is how it will be at the end of time: the angels will appear and separate the wicked from the just to throw them into the blazing furnace where they will be weeping and grinding of teeth.
>
> 'Have you understood all this?' They said, 'Yes.' And he said to them, 'Well then, every scribe who becomes a disciple of the kingdom of heaven is like a householder who brings out from his storeroom things both new and old' (13, 51-52).

That's a very mysterious sentence. What are 'old things and new'? I have pondered that very much. What does it mean to bring forth things old and new?

In my teaching I bring out a lot of old things, and constantly I'm listening to new things. That's not what he means. He means something very deep and profound, which I think only a few people in each generation understand. Teresa of Avila, Catherine of Siena, St. Francis of Assisi, Dorothy Day understood it. I can see why Dorothy Day never wanted to establish an order like I have. Poor woman that I am, I am subject to law and order in some way. Dorothy is subject to holy chaos. She stands out in this century like a pillar of truth, the only American who really understood the new things. She did them herself, and didn't push anyone to do them. She let the chaotic situation that existed among her followers continue. She will be canonized, for she really brought forth what is new and what is old at the same time.

Very few things are new in this world. There were monks in our world long before any church had been established. There were promises made to gods before the Christian era. There was chastity long before we thought about it.

What is it to produce both the new and the old?

It is shedding new ideas about old verities. The Gospel is eternally new. Some people crawl under the words, and because we are led by Jesus Christ or Our Lady, we suddenly know what the words mean from the inside.

ELEVEN
FIRST FRUITS

When you begin to enter into the Gospel, as I said, you have to go under the words, not over the words or at the words; you have to go under, prostrate yourself, and allow the words to cover you, like a cloak or a mantle. You struggle. You struggle terribly with God, or so it seems. I did, and I guess I still do. It's less now.

> When evening came, the disciples went to him and said, 'This is a lonely place, and the time has slipped by; so send the people away, and they can go to the villages to buy themselves some food.' Jesus replied, 'There is no need for them to go; give them something to eat yourselves.' But they answered, 'All we have with us is five loaves and two fishes.' 'Bring them here to me,' he said. He gave orders that the people were to sit down on the grass; then he took the five loaves and two fish, raised his eyes to heaven and said the blessing. And breaking the loaves he handed them to his disciples who gave them to the crowds. They all ate as much as they wanted, and they collected the scraps remaining, twelve baskets full. Those who ate numbered about five thousand men, to say nothing of women and children (14, 15-21).

I often re-read that Gospel when I was hungry. Jesus fed me through other people like the Jewish taxi driver, some stranger, some "Jesus Saves" mission. He assuaged my hunger temporarily. That's why fasting to me is very important. You have to fast for those who are hungry. It's not a question of just fasting during Lent or before the feast of Sts. Peter and

Paul, or on the vigil of great feasts. It's a question of atonement. You can't eat too much when so many people are hungry. I guess that's the reason for my fastings. You see, I take the Gospel at face value.

Now those people were hungry and he gave them to eat. I have the power to give them to eat. I can stir up other people who have money. It all goes together. So often in the evening I see the faces of a thousand hungry people.

Fasting is a very important thing. It really is a mainstay of all religions. It's like a bone structure on which you place the flesh. It's also a beautiful bridge between you and God. God fasted for forty days, and at so many other times. Prayer and fasting reach to the toes of the Lord, of Abba, as my father used to say. My father always used to say that prayer and fasting reach the feet of God.

Fasting is a beautiful thing also because it shows that man is master of himself. It's a counter-balance to technology and wealth. Fasting stands alone with its face turned East, and it says, "Lord, I believe, and I follow you into the deserts and wherever you go."

I realized that when I was starving in Russia. But my hunger in Russia was one thing, whereas in Harlem, Toronto and sometimes in Combermere, fasting is different. When there is *nothing*, that's not fasting. That's starvation and hunger. It's the Third World. But if somebody refrains from eating for the sake of atonement in a country where there is plenty of food, that's an offering. It's a consolation to God. I think it is. It's a discipline of the appetites.

Sometimes I think of it as someone going into a field of flowers, and picking a beautiful blue flower, then a yellow one, a red one, and so forth. And at the end of the day you have a beautiful bouquet you can offer to God. A vase of flowers. Much of the food we eat is unnecessary. For he who fasts for God eats well. It's a very beautiful flower arrangement that you can give to God at night. That's what fasting is to me.

When I look at my old Bible and read about those poor people whom he fed, I feel so glad.

"Directly after this he made the disciples get into the boat and go on ahead to the other side while he would send the crowds away. After sending the crowds away he went up into the hills by himself to pray" (14, 22-23).

That's a very important thing. Always go by yourself to pray.

> When evening came, he was there alone, while the boat, by now far out on the lake, was battling with a heavy sea, for there was a headwind. In the fourth watch of the night he went towards them, walking on the lake, and when the disciples saw him walking on the lake they were terrified. 'It is a ghost,' they said, and cried out in fear. But at once Jesus called out to them, saying, 'Courage! It is I! Do not be afraid.' It was Peter who answered, 'Lord,' he said, 'if it is you, tell me to come to you across the water.' 'Come,' said Jesus. Then Peter got out of the boat and started walking towards Jesus across the water, but as soon as he felt the force of the wind, he took fright and began to sink. 'Lord! Save me!' he cried. Jesus put out his hand at once and held him. 'Man of little faith,' he said, 'why did you doubt?' And as they got into the boat the wind dropped. The men in the boat bowed down before him and said, 'Truly, you are the Son of God' (14, 24-33).

That was a great miracle. But somehow I think Mary Magdalene understood things better. She wasn't looking for any great miracles. She just knelt at his feet, put her head on his knee, and listened and absorbed miracles that were greater than walking on water.

I guess he had to assuage their craving for certainty and do a lot of miracles for them to believe, yet they didn't believe and they crucified him.

I feel sad about that . . . very sad.

I always believed from my childhood, and so did all the people around me, that "touching Christ" can heal. But, there was no question at all about it that it was useless to do any touching unless you had faith.

My mother always said, "Don't bother proclaiming that you believe in God unless you act accordingly. Otherwise nothing will happen except that he is going to get angry with you." And she would quote to me from her old Russian Gospel book: "It is not those who say to me, 'Lord, Lord,' who will enter the kingdom of heaven" (7,21).

And I used to wonder. It was at moments like this that I felt my poverty, even though I was too small to understand what it meant. My mother seemed so wise, so infinitely wise. As for my father, he was wisdom personified.

I remember another time when I was at school in Egypt. Always when we had a Gospel story I could raise my hand and say, "Oh yes, I know, my mother and father do that all the time . . . or do that often . . . or do that sometimes." At an early age I realized that the Gospel had to be lived. Almost before I learned to read and write I knew that these things had to be lived. If they weren't lived, it was no good.

Now here is Matthew talking about the tradition of the Pharisees.

Now that's a pretty powerful answer.

For God said: 'Do your duty to your father and mother and: Anyone who curses father or mother must be put to death.' But you say, 'If anyone says to his father or mother: Anything I have that I might have used to help you is dedicated to God, he is rid of his duty to father or mother.' In this way you have made God's word null and void by means of your tradition. Hypocrites! It was you Isaiah meant when he so rightly prophesized: This people honours me only with lip-service, while their hearts are far from me. The worship they offer me is worthless; the doctrines they teach are only human regulations   (15, 4-9).

This passage pierces my heart. I'm not learned enough to understand its "methodology" — is that the way you say it? I can't divide the words of God into little pieces and examine them with a special method, with a magnifying glass. To me it's a very simple thing. Very simple. It breaks my heart that God had to talk to the Pharisees and Sadducees like that! What they did is very clear. And the same is done today. A man has a good car, a huge house and so forth, while his father and mother live in an old people's home. He says, "I need my car for business." He doesn't need such a big car for business. I watch those big cars pass by and I want to cry. God spoke, but it's as if nobody spoke, and people don't pay any attention.

The disciples, having crossed to the other shore, had forgotten to take any food. Jesus said to them, 'Keep your eyes open, and be on your guard against the yeast of the Pharisees and Sadducees.' And they said to themselves, 'It is because we have not brought any bread.' Jesus knew it, and he said, 'Men of little faith, why are you talking among yourselves about having no bread? Do you not yet understand? Do you not remember the five loaves for the five thousand and the number of baskets you collected? Or the seven loaves for the four thousand and the number of baskets you collected? How could you fail to understand that I was not talking about bread? What I said was: 'Beware of the yeast of the Pharisees and Sadducees.' Then they understood that he was telling them to be on their guard, not against the yeast for making bread, but against the teaching of the Pharisees and Sadducees (16, 5-12).

When you read this Gospel and reread it as I did, you think of the yeast of the Pharisees and the Sadducees. God warned the apostles about it, and they were bemused as always. They were not listening and not hearing. The apostles had a quality of not hearing what they heard, as some of us do. They were worried that they hadn't brought some yeast to make the bread or something like that! In spite of the fact that only the day before they had witnessed the second miracle of the loaves and fishes. And here they are thinking so stupidly. Can you imagine that?

"And they said to themselves, 'It is because we have not brought any bread'" (16:7). They were worried about Jesus being upset because they had no bread. Talk about not listening and not hearing! For me that takes the cake!

So when Jesus told them, "Beware of the yeast of the Pharisees and Sadducees," they FINALLY understood after a long lapse of time, that he was telling them to be on their guard, not against the yeast for making bread, but against the teaching of the Pharisees and Sadducees.

TWELVE

BLIND AND DEAF

No amount of reading the Gospel has dispelled all my darkness. Poor as I am, uneducated in the Scriptures as I am, there are always spots in me that are blind and deaf even though I'm in love with God. You don't have to be rich to be in love with God. Anybody can be in love with God. In fact, everybody should be. What makes me sad is that we're blind and we're deaf.

We don't understand God's ways. And yet he has made the path, his ways, so clear. There is in the Gospel an event that has puzzled me a long time and which always reminds me of the fact that I am indeed blind and deaf. It is found in St. John's Gospel. "On the following day as John stood there again with two of his disciples, Jesus passed, and John stared hard at him and said, 'Look, there is the lamb of God.' Hearing this, the two disciples followed Jesus. Jesus turned around, saw them following and said, 'What do you want?' They answered, 'Rabbi,' — which means Teacher — 'where do you live?' 'Come and see,' he replied; so they went and saw where he lived, and stayed with him the rest of that day. It was about the tenth hour" (1, 35-40).

Only two disciples went to see where he lived. People understood, even in those days when little had yet been revealed about Jesus and when it was dangerous to follow him, that they had to go and see where he lived. Shortly after, they discovered that foxes had holes but he had no place to rest.

From that time Jesus began to make it clear to his

disciples that he was destined to go to Jerusalem and suffer grievously at the hands of the elders and chief priests and scribes, to be put to death and to be raised up on the third day. Then, taking him aside, Peter started to remonstrate with him, 'Heaven preserve you, Lord,' he said, 'this must not happen to you.' But he turned and said to Peter, 'Get behind me, Satan! You are an obstacle in my path, because the way you think is not God's way but man's' (16,21-23).

Now here is our situation. The way we think is man's way, not God's way. The moment you present that picture, you present the whole story of what is happening today, yesterday, and the day before. Instinctively, Peter couldn't conceive that Christ was going to suffer grievously at the hands of the Pharisees and the Sadducees. What does Peter want to do? He wants to protect him, to save him from suffering.

"Then, taking him aside, Peter started to remonstrate with him, 'Heaven preserve you, Lord . . . this must not happen to you.'" Peter thought it just couldn't happen.

But do you ever consider the mixed reaction of the apostles? I often meditate on that because they're my reactions. Since I'm unlearned in the high ways of Scripture, as I told you, I approach **Scripture** from *below* and you know what I see? True, Peter really means well, but when it comes to the final crunch, where is he? He denies Jesus three times. Now take you and me, especially me. Would I be a Magdalen and sit and weep under his cross? Would I be a Veronica and have the courage to wipe his face in front of everybody? Would I be a John, the well-beloved? Good questions!

Fear. Often when I read about God's passion I see the apostles agreeing with Jesus officially and wholeheartedly at the moment. But how sincerely? What happens in the crunch? When the crunch comes we're all marshmallows, all tied up within ourselves, afraid of pain and suffering. We run at the first turn of the thumb-screw, even at the *distant* sound of a hammer upon nails.

> For the Son of Man is going to come in the glory of his Father with his angels, and, when he does, he will reward each one according to his behaviour. I tell you solemnly, there are some of these standing here who will not taste death before they see the Son of Man coming with his kingdom (16, 24-28).

The conditions for following Christ are very simple: "If anyone wants to be a follower of mine, let him renounce himself and take up his cross and follow me" (16:24).

The most difficult part of that text is to renounce yourself. I imagine that taking a cross and following him would be easy if you didn't have to renounce yourself. That Gospel always stops me cold.

The last sentence is certainly a difficult thing to explain: solemnly he says that the people who are around him are going to see him come again. One thousand nine hundred and eighty years later, he has not yet come. "How do you explain that?" I ask myself. "What does it mean to one who looks at the Gospel from the inside, who looks at the words when lying flat on one's back, who looks at the words as they are written by holy hands, but who listens to them especially as they are spoken by God? What do you think of that? Well, it's useless for you to lie. There are moments in the Gospel that leave you blank, my soul!"

Why did he say that? Nearly two thousand years have passed and he hasn't come! There are certain things that I understand very dimly. The Gospel must be preached to everybody, and this must be done and that must be done. We have done none of those things, and we'll never do them. It's a mystery that even lying on your back and looking at the letters from below you cannot solve. So you accept it in the darkness of faith.

> . Six days later, Jesus took with him Peter and James and his brother John and led them up a high mountain where they could be alone. There in their presence he was transfigured: his face shone like the sun and his clothes became as white as the light. Suddenly Moses and Elijah appeared to them; they were talking with him. Then Peter spoke to Jesus. 'Lord,' he said, 'it is wonderful for us to be here; if you wish, I will make three tents here, one for you, one for Moses and one for Elijah. He was still speaking when suddenly a bright cloud covered them with shadow, and from the cloud there came a voice which said, 'This is my Son, the Beloved; he enjoys my favour. Listen to him.' When they heard this, the disciples fell on their faces, overcome with fear. But Jesus came up and touched them. 'Stand up,' he said, 'do not be afraid.' And when they raised their eyes they saw no one but only Jesus (17, 1-8).

That's a fantastic Gospel. It always cheered me up in my poverty, in my loneliness. The Gospel is my companion. Without it I don't think I would have survived.

In this scene of the Transfiguration, only one line means anything to me: "Jesus then came up to them, touched them, and said, 'Stand up, do not be afraid.' And when they raised their eyes they saw no one but only Jesus."

That, to me, is the only thing that matters. In the terrible, horrendous, awful, lonely days of my life, it seemed as if he touched me and I opened my eyes filled with tears and despair. Suddenly, I saw Jesus, and I got up and washed my face and went on about the duty of the moment. That's what the Gospel means to me . . . the duty of the moment. It gives me courage. It gives me food, nourishment, strength, courage, and the ability to keep plugging against every opposition.

> Then the disciples came privately to Jesus. 'Why were we unable to cast it out?' They asked. He answered, 'Because you have little faith. I tell you solemnly, if your faith were the size of a mustard seed you could say to this mountain, "Move from here to there," and it would move; nothing would be impossible for you' (17, 14-20).

When he came down the mountain and found that his disciples had not cured the epileptic, he got quite angry, let me tell you! "Faithless and perverse generation," he called them, "how much longer will I be with you. How much longer must I put up with you?" That's exactly how I feel, alas, about many people. "Bring him to me," said Jesus, and he delivered him from the devil. He went away, but he was tired. He simply told those little pip-squeeks called apostles that they had very little faith.

When I'm by myself I often thank God for the faith he has given me. Because I'm poor, he has given me a faith much bigger than a mustard seed. God takes pity on people like me. He left me on the shores of Canada bereft of everything, pregnant and all the rest, and he took care of me because I believed. There's no denying that: I believed! How many times did I recite the prayer, "Lord, I believe, help my unbelief." "Out of the depths I cry to you, O Lord. Hear the voice of my supplications." Those were the prayers I said year after year after year. I still do.

> One day when they were together in Galilee, Jesus said to them, 'The Son of Man is going to be handed over into the power of men; they will put him to death, and on the third day he will be raised to life again.' And a great sadness came over them (17, 22-23).

He gives the second prophecy of his passion. At least something sensible comes over them. They're sad for the first time. You'd think they would have been sad before! That's another thing I find so related to life. We're sad, those of us who are able to be sad with others, or to put it another way, "Blessed are those who mourn." To mourn is to share the sadness of others. They certainly are blessed who do that.

> At this time the disciples came to Jesus and said, 'Who is the greatest in the kingdom of heaven?' So he called a little child to him and set the child in front of him. Then he said, 'I tell you solemnly, unless you change and become like little children you will never enter the kingdom of heaven. And so, the one who makes himself as little as this little child is the greatest in the kingdom of heaven (18, 1-4).

Those disciples were just like us. We always ask metaphysical questions. "Who is the greatest in the kingdom of God?" Now isn't that a stupid question? Each one wanted him to say, "You." They were only thinking about themselves. God knocked them for a loop. He brought a child and said, "I tell you solemnly, unless you change and become like little children you will never enter the kingdom of heaven. And so, the one who makes himself as little as this little child is the greatest in the kingdom of heaven."

Now *that* I have always understood. When people are like children they have to accept hand-outs. A child accepts hand-outs for a long time — in school, at home, everywhere.

THIRTEEN

HE SPOKE ON DIVORCE

I was always astonished at the fact that Jesus was constantly surrounded by people. Has this ever struck you?

In this nineteenth chapter of St. Matthew we read that he left Galilee. But before going into that I'd like to say that when you preach the Gospel you get a strange sense of being lifted up, almost bodily. I wouldn't say levitating, because I never levitated, but it's as if I was really lifted up, higher and higher, and I came closer to the Trinity.

To be perfectly frank, I never thought that I would be a little afraid to preach "The Gospel of a Poor Woman," but I am. Because when we deal with the lofty thoughts that Christ speaks about, and listen to the simple words that he used to explain all our problems, it kind of frightens you a little bit.

He leaves Galilee and he's off to Judea which is, as you know, on the far side of the Jordan. He was not too happy with the Galileans, nor they with him. No sooner does he reach the other side of the Jordan than the Pharisees and Sadducees immediately put him between the devil and the deep blue sea, or they want to roast him on a hot fire. Here they come, you can just see them, proud of heart, arrogant of bearing, looking through everybody as if they were no more than mosquitoes or ants. Those characters, I never liked them! I had a great difficulty with them when reading the Gospel. I guess that when you're poor and uneducated, it takes time before you understand that you have to love even the Sadducees and Pharisees.

It certainly is hard! But out of that comes the realization that you have to love everybody. The grocer around the corner may look just like a Pharisee. If you ask him for the price of soap, for instance, he may give you this supercilious look and say, "Madam, it's right there written on the shelf. Even though it's written on the package we still write them on the shelf." And when he turns his back you feel that he meant to add, "for idiots like you." Well, who says that I'm not an idiot? I am poor, so I'm glad to know the price of soap. But we're not talking about soap. We're talking about God.

Those Pharisees approached him right there and then. And what did they do? They tested him.

"Is it against the Law for a man to divorce his wife on any pretext whatever?" (19,3).

Can you imagine those characters? They were always negative, never positive. There are lots of people like them. Don't you, my dear readers, know people who are always negative in their questions and never satisfied with any answers? They find nothing good to say, like those characters here, I mean the Sadducees and Pharisees.

> He answered, 'Have you not read that the Creator from the beginning made them male and female and that he said: This is why a man must leave father and mother, and cling to his wife, and the two become one body? They are no longer two, therefore, but one body. So then, what God has united, man must not divide' (19, 4-6).

I read this often throughout my life. I had reason to think about it. I had to go through an annulment of my first marriage. It was so difficult and so very,

very painful. By granting an annulment the Church declares that a marriage is null and void and that both parties are free to re-marry. Yes, that's true. They married in good faith and they separate in good faith, with the permission of the Church. And yet one does not easily accept that the union which once existed is now broken. One does not easily forget!

But I'm walking away from what God said. He said very simply, " . . . what God has united, man must not divide."

> They said to him, 'Then why did Moses command that a writ of dismissal should be given in cases of divorce?' 'It was because you were so unteachable,' he said, 'that Moses allowed you to divorce your wives, but it was not like this from the beginning. Now I say this to you: the man who divorces his wife — I am not speaking of fornication — and marries another, is guilty of adultery' (19, 7-9).

Well, I meditated on that very much. And do you know something? When I finally got the annulment, sorrow stretched its hands out and took my heart and squeezed it. What happens to a squeezed heart, not to the physical organ but to that mysterious spiritual organ which bleeds when we are hurt? I started thinking of all the broken people, the broken homes and families. I could literally see the gnarled and old hands of sorrow squeeze human hearts until they bled. So much of that happens today. Isn't that terrible? When I read about divorces I want to cry, don't you?

Jesus' answer really didn't quite register even with the disciples! His ideas didn't always register right away. He often had to explain (which should cheer us up, those of us who try to preach the Gospel.) You have to explain a lot.

"The disciples said to him, 'If that is how things

are between husband and wife, it is not advisable to marry'" (19,10).

Well, they had a point there, humanly speaking. I'm not going into that. Anybody who reads the Gospel of a woman who is poor can think of thousands of little towns or villages where the poor are found, and remember the terrible lives that some couples live . . . terrible lives! And lift your eyes and look at the *palaces.* It's the same wherever you look.

> But he replied, 'It is not everyone who can accept what I have said, but only those to whom it is granted. There are eunuchs born that way from their mother's womb, there are eunuchs made so by men, and there are eunuchs who have made themselves that way for the sake of the kingdom of heaven. Let anyone accept this who can' (19, 11-12).

Now that is really hard. I meditated on this endlessly. As you know, the Lord gave me Eddie as a second husband. But very soon he took Eddie away through our vow of celibacy. So I was very interested in that answer of Jesus. It's very important for us in our apostolate, and it's very important for all the apostolates that are interested in celibacy.

Quite a few of my young readers may not know what a eunuch is. A eunuch is a castrated man. When we castrate dogs and other animals, they become utterly uninterested in sex. Among the Muslims, for example, such men took care of the pasha's harem. Some Muslims may still have eunuchs.

Jesus said, "There are eunuchs born that way from their mother's womb . . . . " For some it's a birth defect. And then he said that there are some who make themselves eunuchs. That is to say, nothing is done to their body. No. But because they're in love with God and God was a virgin, and because he spoke this beautiful sentence, " . . . and there are eunuchs who have made themselves that way for the sake of the kingdom of heaven," they decide to live in complete celibacy.

Isn't that beautiful? So that they are only busy about the kingdom of heaven. "Let any man accept this who can." It's a free invitation.

Jesus Speaks to Many

I was just thinking of all the kids I have known — scrawny kids of the slums of Harlem and of many other places. I don't know why my thoughts turn to them today. Perhaps it's because I was thinking about Judas.

Today is Wednesday of Holy Week, and on this day the Eastern churches remember Judas' kiss. People fast because of it. I was thinking of Judas and for some reason I was thinking about him as a child. What kind of a child was he? Strange thoughts, but perhaps suitable for Holy Week.

So I opened the Gospel of St. Matthew and here was Jesus talking about children. The apostles didn't want the children to bother him but he said,

"Let the little children alone, and do not stop them coming to me; for it is to such as these that the kingdom of heaven belongs" (19, 14-15).

Now, that's very nice. The first thing he does is tell the apostles to let the children come to him. And I said to myself, "We have in Russia a saying, 'Who takes in a child, takes in Christ.'" Because of that saying, we didn't have too many orphanages. People took children in. They also cared for the elderly, because any stranger you harbored was Jesus Christ. Children have to be loved in a way that they can understand.

I was thinking of Friendship House Toronto. We had 700 children in Toronto, and we had 400 in Harlem. And they all loved us, the little ones and the big ones. We managed!

And I was content. I read this Gospel again and I said to myself, "Well, as far as children are concerned, whenever you had to take care of them, you did," and I felt happy, I must admit.

Then the Gospel swung to the rich man. Funny, the children and the rich man! He said that people who were as little children would get into heaven. Now what about this rich young man? Well, this is worth reading, you know, and pondering because it's not that simple.

And there was a man who came to him and asked, 'Master, what good deed must I do to possess eternal life?' Jesus said to him, 'Why do you ask me about what is good? There is one alone who is good. But if you wish to enter into life, keep the commandments.' He said, 'Which?' Jesus replied, 'You must not kill. You must not commit adultery. You must not bring false witness. Honour your father and mother, and: you must love your neighbour as yourself.' The young man said to him, 'I have kept all these. What more do I need to do?' Jesus said, 'If you wish to be perfect, go and sell what you own and give the money to the poor, and you will have treasure in heaven; then come, follow me.' But when the young man heard these words he went away sad, for he was a man of great wealth (19, 16-22).

That's what Matthew writes, can you imagine, right after the little children! I still see them, scrawny, with torn shirts and pants in all those slums, and yet looking for love. You would think that Matthew would put this incident of the rich man a little later, but no, here he is right at the end of the incident with the children. It is well that that is so. I thought it over after awhile.

This passage about the rich young man has been the focal point of my life. "Go and sell what you own . . . !" That was said to the rich man. And it was said to me, when, after being very poor, I had become rich. God didn't like that. It was obvious, positively obvious to me, that I had to become poor. There it was. He was talking to the rich man about the commandments. The man said, "I have kept all these." And I could say that I kept them, too.

I had been poor, very poor, and then suddenly, through the lecture bureau and one thing or another, I earned a lot of money. $20,000 a year was a lot of money in those days. But that wasn't what God wanted me to do. God wanted me to be the rich man who gave it all up. It took me quite a while to get the point. And I said to myself, "Yes, that's the way God wants it. He gave me a chance to earn this money so that I would have a chance to give it up." I had a choice. I had been poor. I knew poverty very well from every angle. I had been a beggar; I knew what it meant to live on a pittance as a laundress, as a waitress.

So I knew poverty. Then suddenly he gave me wealth. Why do you think he did that? Obviously for one reason: That I might give it up. He just wanted me to have the pleasure and the joy of giving it up for him. It's like Eddie, my second husband. God gave me Eddie for a little while and then he gave me celibacy for so many years. I think God plays little games with me, I don't know. But I'm glad I'm poor again and I don't own anything. In this house where I am now, nothing belongs to me. It all belongs to Madonna House. Isn't that nice?

Yes, it's good to be poor. I was reading that Gospel again and I was feeling sad for the rich man, and evidently so was Christ.

> Then Jesus said to his disciples, 'I tell you solemnly, it will be hard for a rich man to enter the kingdom of heaven. Yes, I tell you again, it is easier for a camel to pass through the eye of a needle than for a rich man to enter the kingdom of heaven.' When the disciples heard this they were astonished. 'Who can be saved, then?' they said. Jesus gazed at them. 'For men,' he told them, 'this is impossible; for God everything is possible' (19, 23-26).

Well now, this is a pretty smart idea, "all things are possible to God." One evening I stepped out of my little cabin on the island and looked at Madonna House across the swamp. There was the white snow, just like in Russia. I saw a big house, and beyond it many other houses. Then it hit me, it REALLY hit me, that poverty becomes wealth when you hand everything over to God and place it all into the crucified hands of Christ that can hold nothing. When you gather up all that you possess, and offer it to him, his Father takes it and, lo and behold, you're poor, and you are identified with Christ, not with all the rich people. You don't need to worry about the eyes of needles because you won't have to pass through anything.

So it became quite clear to me that with God everything is possible. Looking across the river at our main house and at the other houses, I realized that God had made a *village* of Madonna House without using any money of ours whatsoever. In poverty was wealth because we had given everything to God.

So I kept on reading. Here was Peter coming along:

> Then Peter spoke. 'What about us?' he said to him. 'We have left everything and followed you. What are we to

have, then?' Jesus said to him, 'I tell you solemnly, when all is made new and the Son of Man sits on his throne of glory, you will yourselves sit on twelve thrones to judge the twelve tribes of Israel. And everyone who has left houses, brothers, sisters, father, mother, children or land for the sake of my name will be repaid a hundred times over, and also inherit eternal life. Many who are first will be last, and the last, first' (19, 27-30).

That is one of the passages that I love very, very much because it really enters your heart and makes you face what poverty is. Here I am, a woman who is poor, trying to talk about the Gospel through my poverty. But do you understand something? Because I approach the Gospel in utter simplicity and poverty, it too becomes enriched. And I understand it, maybe not with my head so much as with my heart. Now take these words.

"And everyone who has left houses, brothers, sisters, father, mother, children or land for the sake of my name will be repaid a hundred times over, and also inherit eternal life" (19,29).

The land that I love, Russia, I have given up. A bit of it lies in a cellophane bag behind Our Lady's icon in my log cabin. The love of a Russian for his land is really something extraordinary; I'm an exile, or refugee. Of course, it wasn't my idea, but God asked me through the Revolution to give up Russia, and I did. I became like him, a refugee, not in Egypt, but in America.

Then he asked me to give up my husband and my son. All this I have done.

And that brings me a tremendous understanding of people. I told you if you look at the Gospel from below, sort of passing under the words — like in the Eastern Rite on Good Friday you pass under the shroud — if you lie down humbly — if you look at the Gospel from below, you understand the infinite wealth of what happens when you really follow Jesus. When you give up your husband, you can console husbands and wives all over the world, because you know the sacrifices involved. Eddie and I were able to console an awful lot of people, which we could never have done if we hadn't given each other to God.

Then, if you give up children, brothers, sisters, lo and behold, you have more brothers and sisters than you ever dreamed of! Hundreds! Thousands! Because everybody becomes your brother or sister when you have given your own up for God's sake. Do you understand? A fantastic wealth is yours. You suddenly realize, "My God, I haven't given up anything. I've received everything." Do you follow what I say? (I really don't know if it's a good idea to write about this Gospel or not because it's all a hodge-podge of my funny ideas, but that's how I feel.) This is a glad paragraph. Glad, because it shows that, indeed, for God, all things are possible. When you do the impossible for him, he does the impossible for you.

And here is another very interesting sentence: "Many who are first will be last, and the last, first." That's something to understand, eh? Maybe some Pope who was first will be last, and some prostitute will be first. It all depends on the heart. Do you know what I mean? That sentence is a "hope" sentence. It belongs to the theology of the virtue of hope.

FOURTEEN
JESUS CONTINUES TO PREACH

Yes, Christ continues to preach, and always in parables. It makes you feel good, symbols and parables! I love a symbol and I love a parable.

"Now the kingdom of heaven is like a landowner going out at daybreak to hire workers for his vineyard" (20,1).

In Friendship House, New York, we often had women come around ten o'clock to rest their weary feet and to share a cup of coffee, if we could spare it. They came from the Bronx across the bridge. They were the ones who had not been hired. Every morning between 7 and 10, in the days of the Depression, forty or fifty black women went to the corner of 126th Street, just across the bridge. Rich people went there and hired them for a day's work.

As I passed them on my way to Mass, I had great qualms of conscience, because it seemed to me that they weren't for hire at all. They were for slavery. For some reason I saw blocks set up on that street, slave blocks, and people sold. Do you know what those ladies in the big cars that stopped to "buy them" or hire them offered them per day? Think. You never would guess. 50 cents! 50 cents a day! It's not enough to feed anybody. And they had to pay their own fare back! Christ must have thought of those women when he told this parable.

He made an agreement with the workers for one denarius a day, and sent them to his vineyard. Going out at about the third hour he saw others standing

idle in the market place and said to them, 'You go to
my vineyard too and I will give you a fair wage.' So
they went. At about the sixth hour and again at about
the ninth hour, he went out and did the same. Then at
about the eleventh hour he went out and found more
men standing around, and he said to them, 'Why have
you been standing here idle all day?' 'Because no one
has hired us,' they answered. He said to them, 'You go
into my vineyard, too.' In the evening, the owner of the
vineyard said to his bailiff, 'Call the workers and pay
them their wages, starting with the last arrivals and
ending with the first.' So those who were hired at
about the eleventh hour came forward and received
one denarious each. When the first came, they ex-
pected to get more, but they too received one denarious each. They took it, but grumbled at the
landowner. 'The men who came last,' they said, 'have
done only one hour, and you have treated them all the
same as us, though we have done a heavy day's work in
all the heat.' He answered one of them and said, 'My
friend, I am not being unjust to you; did we not agree
on one denarious? Take your earnings and go. I choose
to pay the last-comer as much as I pay you. Have I no
right to do what I like with my own? Why be envious
because I am generous?' Thus the last will be first, and
the first, last' (20, 2-16).

Again we get this picture that the last will be first
and the first last. It recurs again and again throughout
the Gospel. So we had better watch out! I'm reminded
of "Give Me That Stranger," a Good Friday song of
the Eastern Rite:

When he saw that the sun had hidden its rays, and
that the veil of the temple was rent as the Saviour died,
Joseph went to Pilate, pleaded with him and cried out:
    Give me that Stranger
    Who since his youth
    Had wandered as a stranger.
    Give me that Stranger

Killed in hatred by his own people
as a Stranger.

Give me that Stranger
Upon whom I look with wonder
Seeing him a Guest of Death.

Give me that Stranger
Whom envious men
Estranges from the world.

Give me that Stranger
That I may bury him in a tomb,
Who being a stranger has no place
Whereon to lay his head.

Give me that Stranger
To whom his mother cried out
As she saw him dead:
'My Son, my senses are wounded
And my heart is burned
As I see You dead!
Yet, trusting in your resurrection,
I magnify You!'

In such words did the honorable Joseph plead with
Pilate. He took the Saviour's body and, with fear,
wrapped it in linen with spices. And placed You in a
Tomb, O You who grant everlasting life and great
mercy to us all! (Most Reverend Joseph Raya and Jose
de Vinck, *Byzantine Daily Worship* Allendale, N.J.,
Alleluia Press, 1969, p. 833.)

There is a tenderness about this parable, a compassion. I used to read it when I was out of work and
had to go out and look for a job and my feet were tired
and I couldn't get a job. I used to cheer myself up
thinking that maybe someone would come at the
eleventh hour. And Somebody did come to console me
and give me another job to do for him, an inner job, a
spiritual job. Jesus Christ came, consoled me and said,
"Now, Catherine, you can do something for me." And
I would say, "What can I do for you, dear Lord?" And

he would say, "Well, you can offer me a day without work. It's been tough, hasn't it?" And I would say, "It certainly has!" "And nobody came to hire you at the eleventh hour except me who came to console you but not to hire you for you are already hired out to me. You see, I hired you long ago and far away, if 'hire' is the word. Yes, today you accepted your lack of food, for you have no money, and your feet are tired. They were my feet. And because you thought of me, this day of yours has gone wherever I wanted to put it. I could bend down and give a piece of it to some poor person here. I could bend down and give another piece to somebody else over there. Did you know about that, Catherine?" I said, "No, I didn't," because I didn't quite understand it all. Anyhow, it was sort of a consoling discussion with God at the eleventh hour, for I had many a day when I couldn't find any job. So I understood all about the eleventh hour.

Jesus began to talk about his passion to his disciples.

> Jesus was going up to Jerusalem, and on the way he took the Twelve to one side and said to them, 'Now we are going up to Jerusalem, and the Son of Man is about to be handed over to the chief priests and scribes. They will condemn him to death and will hand him over to the pagans to be mocked and scourged and crucified; and on the third day he will rise again' (20, 17-19).

Well, I'm telling you, that too is a paragraph that I know. For in Toronto I was delivered (just as he said he would be delivered) to the public to be crucified. "The Son of Man is about to be handed over to the chief priests." Certainly if I was ever handed over to the priests, believe you me, it was in Friendship House, Toronto. I was accused of being a Communist by priests and nuns, and my work collapsed. I had to leave, and I was handed over to the pagans to be mocked and scourged and crucified. Well, I should say, that I was handed over, not to the pagans, but to the Christians. It's the Christians who crucified me. So you see, in a very small measure, I understand the words of Jesus because my hands have been crucified, my feet have been crucified, my heart was pierced with a lance.

> Then the mother of Zebedee's sons came with her sons to make a request of him, and bowed low; and he said to her, 'What is it you want?' She said to him, 'Promise that these two sons of mine may sit one at your right hand the other at your left in your kingdom.' 'You do not know what you are asking,' Jesus answered. 'Can you drink the cup that I am going to drink?' They replied, 'We can.' 'Very well,' he said, 'you shall drink my cup, but as for seats at my right hand and my left, these are not mine to grant; they belong to those to whom they have been allotted by my Father' (20, 20-23).

Now, I don't like this woman of Zebedee. She wants her sons to have a higher place than all the other ten, period! I don't like her. But I pray for her. On second thought, she is in heaven, so I don't need to pray for her. She's okay.

Now, there is one thing here that interests me. He says, "Can you drink the cup that I am going to drink?" And they say they can. And he says, yes, they will drink it, but as to where they will sit it is not for him to grant. He told them they would drink his cup, and so they did, because they died martyrs. To drink his cup is to be a martyr. Sometimes you find martyrdom right next to you, in daily, ordinary life.

I remember a poem I wrote in French:

Reponse

Vous me chantez une belle chanson
Dont les paroles en paraboles
étaient cachées
Mais j'ai les clefs des mots cachés
Je ne chante pas, moi. Mais je vous fais
cadeau — de mots. Car vous aussi
avez été donné ces clefs!
Vous dites, Je suis un
Bohémien — et Bohémien je vais rester?

Ecoutez:

Je suis Lépreuse — une femme transfigurée
blessée — laide — de la laideur
de Crucifié!
Je suis l'enfant abandonné
La pucelle profanée
La vieille pauvre insultée
Je suis tous les clochards
Les vauriens — les rejetés!
Je suis lépreuse

Je suis malade — tous les malades
Sur tous les grabats dans toutes
les maisons délabrées, condamnées
dan nos villes prostituées!

Je suis le Crucifié d'un amour —
que rien ne peut soulager
Excepté la rencontre
l'amier dans l'autre
Bohémienne je suis née
Bohémienne je suis restée

Mais maintenant je suis changée
Mes nuits sont blanches —
Mes jours — brisés.

So there is a bloody martyrdom, when you must drink the cup in one swallow, while the blood is flowing from a wound inflicted by this or that terrorist. And there is another cup that's slowly poured out, drop by drop.

Then he leaves Mrs. Zebedee there and continues:

> When the other ten heard this they were indignant with the two brothers. But Jesus called them to him and said, 'You know that among the pagans the rulers lord it over them, and their great men make their authority felt. This is not to happen among you. No; anyone who wants to be great among you must be your servant, and anyone who wants to be first among you must be your slave, just as the Son of Man came not to be served but to serve, and to give his life as a ransom for many' (20, 24-28).

That's what we should be, or strive to be, the servant of all. But we want to dominate.

Leadership through service really goes against the grain. We don't like that. We don't mind *being* served. We don't even mind serving the poor officially, on a committee. We certainly like giving a couple of bucks for the poor, and serve on a committee for the old ladies, the retarded, the crippled children. It doesn't interfere with what I want to do, with my way of life. Definitely and positively we do not wish to do the will of God.

Now, it's clear what the Son of Man did. We have to do the same. But we don't want to because that is hard, and not only hard, it takes away from us the feeling that we are in charge. He who thinks he is in charge of himself, well, there is only one character who can put that into your head. It's the devil. He mixes everything up, making a mish-mash of our lives. He says, "You are in charge of everything." In other words, making an idol of yourself.

We're so saintly that God forbid we should pray to an idol! Oh no, we don't go around praying in front of any idols. So we think! Maybe we don't make little men out of plasticene like children do, and then stand in front of them and adore them, but what about power and money and prestige? Of course we are full of **idolatry!**

God knows it's bad enough to adore power and wealth and prestige, but to adore YOURSELF, that's our greatest idolatry.

Once you begin to adore yourself, you're finished. You're nobody, because, once you're in the power of Satan you become a blob, just a blob!

> As they left Jericho a large crowd followed him. Now there were two blind men sitting at the side of the road. When they heard that it was Jesus who was passing by, they shouted, 'Lord! Have pity on us, Son of David.' And the crowd scolded them and told them to keep quiet, but they only shouted more loudly, 'Lord! Have pity on us, Son of David.' Jesus stopped, called them over and said, 'What do you want me to do for you?' They said to him, 'Lord, let us have our sight back.' Jesus felt pity for them and touched their eyes, and immediately their sight returned and they followed him (20, 29-34).

They asked him to cure them of blindness. At first nobody wanted to allow them to come to Jesus. This is what happens to so many young people today, and to adults also. They're being hindered in their attempt to reach Christ. There are all kinds of things pulling them away — TM, yoga, sensitivity groups. Then they yelled loud enough for him to hear and he comes and says, "What can I do for you?" And they say, "Give us our sight."

Now the first thing to notice is that they have faith. They yell above the noise of the crowd, and they continue yelling for him. Because they have faith they are cured. That's very important. When you are in a crowd of your peers, stand out, yell, move towards God, don't move towards your peers.

As soon as he cured them, what did they do? They followed him. They weren't like the nine lepers who all went away. These to whom he gave sight followed him. And since he gives us sight, we too should follow him!

Faith and Prayer

Somehow or other I have reached the twenty-first chapter of St. Matthew. How I did it, I don't know, but speaking generally, it is easy to talk of my beloved Gospels. Yes, easy, because it's consoling. It always consoles me. But here, in the 21st Chapter, what does Jesus do? It says the Messiah enters Jerusalem.

> When they were near Jerusalem and had come in sight of Bethphage on the Mount of Olives, Jesus sent two disciples, saying to them, 'Go to the village facing you, and you will immediately find a tethered donkey and a colt with her. Untie them and bring them to me. If anyone says anything to you, you are to say, 'The Master needs them and will send them back directly.' This took place to fulfill the prophecy: Say to the daughter of Zion: Look, your king comes to you; he is humble, he rides on a donkey and on a colt, the foal of a beast of burden (21, 1-5).

So I said to myself, as I was re-reading this Gospel, "Why does it always thrill you so?" And I came to the conclusion that the thrill comes from the prophecy of the Old Testament. Listen to that again: "Look, your king comes to you; he is humble, he rides on a donkey and on a colt, the foal of a beast of burden."

Well, talk of humility! He could have had a beautiful Arab steed in Palestine, with a flaming mane. I remember an Arab steed in my childhood. It was brought to father to see. It was a reddish-brown colour, and it had a red mane, literally, and the sun was shining and the mane was glorious. But no, Jesus didn't ride any kind of thoroughbred horse. No. He took a donkey, a beast of burden. When I am full of big ideas, it's good for me to read the 21st Chapter of St. Matthew. It makes me abruptly confront the things that are hidden somewhere in my heart. And I cry out to the Lord to cleanse them.

He continues: "So the disciples went out and did as Jesus had told them" (21,6). The disciples went out and did as Jesus told them. Suddenly in my mind I recall the Transfiguration. "When they looked up they saw no one but Jesus." He told them to do something, and without any questions they did it. So I said to myself, "My poverty is very rich because I do the will of God." At least I try to. And I love in faith, which is his gift. And how can you be poor when you have these things? So in my poverty I become wealthy.

He continues:

So the disciples went out and did as Jesus had told them. They brought the donkey and the colt, then they laid their cloaks on their backs and he sat on them. Great crowds of people spread their cloaks on the road, while others were cutting branches from the streets and spreading them in his path. The crowds who went in front of him and those who followed were all shouting: 'Hosanna to the Son of David! Blessings on him who comes in the name of the Lord! Hosanna in the highest heavens!' And when he entered Jerusalem, the whole city was in turmoil. 'Who is this?' people asked, and the crowds answered, 'This is the prophet Jesus from Nazareth in Galilee' (21, 6-11).

When I read that Gospel, I'm happy, happy because somebody finally rendered him homage. But I also have a sense of sadness, tremendous sadness. Why don't people render homage to God as the children and

the people of Jerusalem did? Many Christians do not
render homage to God and to Jesus Christ. I don't care
if they are Protestant or Catholic or what-have-you.
Many have thrown him out of their lives. No hosannas,
no palms, nothing. And I feel sad. The shadow of the
crucifix hangs over me. Then I remember that my
mother told me that I was born under the shadow of
the Cross. Then I remember what Archbishop Neil
McNeil told me, that I would suffer much, but to
persevere in the apostolate. I remember what the Pope
said to me: "No matter what the price, Madam, you
must persevere, for the Church is about to endure great
difficulties."

My mind goes back, back, back, to the Russian
hermit in Solovetsk, a monastery in the north of
Russia, now changed into a concentration camp.
During the civil war in Russia we happened to visit that
monastery. It so happened that a hermit returned to
the monastery after he had spent thirty years alone in
his hermitage. The Abbot permitted my husband and I
to go to this holy man for a blessing. When I knelt
before him he looked at me deeply with his light blue
eyes and said, "You will go very far into the Spirit and
you will suffer much, and you will be a staff to many."
In my utter poverty I thought about that, in terms of
this Gospel. The people proclaimed, "This is the
prophet Jesus from Nazareth in Galilee." That's what
I have to do; I have to proclaim Jesus that everyone
may know that I belong to Jesus. But he had all of
Jerusalem in turmoil!

> Jesus then went into the Temple and drove out all
> those who were selling and buying there; he upset the
> tables of the money changers and the chairs of those
> who were selling pigeons. 'According to scripture,' he
> said, 'my house will be called a house of prayer; but

you are turning it into a robber's den.' There were also
blind and lame people who came to him in the Temple,
and he cured them. At the sight of the wonderful things
he did and of the children shouting, 'Hosanna to the
Son of David' in the Temple, the chief priests and the
scribes were indignant. 'Do you hear what they are
saying?' they said to him. 'Yes,' Jesus answered, 'have
you never read this: By the mouths of children, babes
in arms, you have made sure of praise?' With that he
left them and went out of the city to Bethany where he
spent the night (21, 12-16).

There you are. Jesus didn't cow-tow to those VIPs
at all. With his words he cut them like a sword, right
where it hurt. He knew where he was going. He knew
they would soon condemn him. As I re-read this
Gospel, I see myself, after trying to get a Negro into
Fordham University, a Jesuit college, and coming
home and crying on the floor in my poor room because
they wouldn't accept him. In how many colleges of all
kinds of Orders did I try to get Negroes accepted
during the late thirties to no avail. Collegeville,
Minnesota accepted them, and the Madames of the
Sacred Heart in Manhattanville — these alone of all
the colleges in America. It was so difficult, so difficult.

In struggling for racial justice, as I look back, I see
that in some small way I too faced a few VIPs, and I
didn't shrink from telling the truth about inter-racial
justice. But I wept a lot in private. I wonder if Christ
did the same.

Matthew goes on:

As he was returning to the city in the early morning,
he felt hungry. Seeing a fig tree by the road, he went up
to it and found nothing on it but leaves. And he said to
it, 'May you never bear fruit again'; and at that instant
the fig tree withered. The disciples were amazed when
they saw it. 'What happened to the tree,' they said,

'that it withered there and then?' Jesus answered, 'I tell you solemnly, if you have faith and do not doubt at all, not only will you do what I have done to the fig tree but even if you say to this mountain, "Get up and throw yourself into the sea," it will be done. And if you have faith, everything you ask for in prayer you will receive' (21, 18-22).

We have a farm, a handicraft center, a Madonna House. I stand on my little balcony at home and look across the river. I don't believe my eyes. I might well not believe them because they're not my eyes, they're God's eyes. I mean, what I see was done by God. If you have faith you will receive everything you ask for in prayer.

He had gone into the Temple and was teaching, when the chief priests and the elders of the people came to him and said, 'What authority have you for acting like this? And who gave you this authority?' 'And I,' replied Jesus, 'will ask you a question, only one; if you tell me the answer to it, I will then tell you my authority for acting like this. John's baptism: where did it come from: heaven or man?' And they argued it out this way among themselves. 'If we say from heaven, he will retort, "Then why did you refuse to believe him?"'; but if we say from man, we have the people to fear, for they all hold that John was a prophet.' So their reply to Jesus was, 'We do not know,' and he retorted, 'Nor will I tell you my authority for acting like this' (21, 23-27).

That's the kind of thing I have to face all the time, around, around, around the mulberry bush. There are members of the community and other people who always want to get out from under. You should hear the logical answers! I'm afraid of logical answers because the devil has the most logical answers. God is a risk, but the devil never risks. He's always certain.

Matthew continues:

There was a man, a landowner, who planted a vine-yard; he fenced it round, dug a winepress in it and built a tower; then he leased it to tenants and went abroad. When vintage time drew near he sent his servants to the tenants to collect his produce. But the tenants seized his servants, thrashed one, killed another and stoned a third. Next he sent some more servants, this time a larger number, and they dealt with them in the same way. Finally he sent his son to them. 'They will respect my son,' he said. But when the tenants saw the son, they said to each other, 'This is the heir. Come on, let us kill him and take over his inheritance.' So they seized him and threw him out of the vineyard and killed him. Now when the owner of the vineyard comes, what will he do to those tenants?' They answered, 'He will bring those wretches to a wretched end and lease the vineyard to other tenants who will deliver the produce to him when the season arrives.' Jesus said to them, 'Have you never read in the scriptures: It was the stone rejected by the builders that became the keystone. This was the Lord's doing and it is wonderful to see? I tell you, then, that the kingdom of God will be taken from you and given to a people who will produce its fruit.'

When they heard his parables, the chief priests and the scribes realized he was speaking about them, but though they would have liked to arrest him they were afraid of the crowds, who looked on him as a prophet (21, 33-46).

That's a very powerful thing. I don't read this paragraph very often because it's a tough one. In my poverty I sorrow over that paragraph. It is Christ the Father sent. The vineyard is *us,* and he sent a lot of prophets and they were all stoned. And he sent his own Son, and we crucified him. Of course, I realize he is the cornerstone. I don't like seeing him crucified, and so I sorrow over this paragraph.

I think Jesus Christ sorrowed too. Whenever I

mention it to him (and I mention it often), he answers sometimes. I kind of talk to Jesus Christ via the Gospel.

FIFTEEN

THE GREATEST COMMANDMENT OF ALL

I was surprised that in my reading I had reached the 22nd chapter of Matthew, where he talks about the parable of the wedding feast. This is what he says:

> Jesus began to speak to them in parables once again, 'The kingdom of heaven may be compared to a king who gave a feast for his son's wedding. He sent his servants to call those who had been invited, but they would not come' (22, 1-2).

It makes me think of so many people whom God invites to his table but they don't come, especially today. There are so many that don't even go to Mass and receive the Body and Blood of Christ nor drink of his limpid waters. Sad, isn't it? At least I felt terribly sad as I read the beginning of this parable. It goes on:

> He sent his servants to call those who had been invited, but they would not come. Next he sent some more servants, 'Tell those who have been invited,' he said, 'that I have my banquet all prepared, my oxen and fattened cattle have been slaughtered, everything is ready. Come to the wedding.' But they were not interested; one went off to his farm, another to his business, and the rest seized his servants, maltreated them and killed them (22, 3-6).

Well that's what's happening now in the world. In his infinite compassion and love, God the Father invites everybody to come to the wedding feast of his Son and the **Church,** through which we receive the Sacraments. So few come. So terribly few care! It's getting better now, as I look around, but not much. I think it's time to pray very much for our priests, bishops, nuns, our laity, everybody. This parable always makes me feel sad. I don't know why, but it does.

> The king was furious. He despatched his troops, destroyed those murderers and burnt their town. Then he said to his servants, 'The wedding is ready; but as those who were invited proved to be unworthy, go to the crossroads in the town and invite everyone you can find to the wedding.' So these servants went out on to the roads and collected together everyone they could find, bad and good alike; and the wedding hall was filled with guests. When the king came in to look at the guests he noticed one man who was not wearing a wedding garment, and said to him, 'How did you get in here, my friend, without a wedding garment?' And the man was silent. Then the king said to the attendants, 'Bind him hand and foot and throw him out into the dark, where there will be weeping and grinding of teeth.' For many are called, but few are chosen (22, 7-14).

I have never understood this. One of these days I'll find a priest who will explain to me what it means. He's inviting everybody, right? Obviously not everybody can buy a wedding garment. Here comes some kind of hobo. Is the Lord expecting this man to buy a wedding garment? Is he supposed to *own* a wedding garment? Some baptismal robes? It kind of confuses me, you know.

And not only that, but the poor guy is thrown out into hell! I wondered, what does that all mean? Suppose that I came in there and I had no wedding garment, what would happen to me? I would go to hell? Now what have I done to go to hell? Just because I had no wedding garment. I don't get that. Of course, I'm a poor woman and I don't study much, but I must admit I don't know what that means. I have never understood it. So there it is. Maybe some priest will read this and will explain it to me. Somebody will tell me. You can't expect me to know everything! I don't know much. This is a poor woman's Gospel.

"Many are called but few are chosen." Can you imagine that? The only reason few are chosen is because they are not worthy. But he himself asked them to go into the highways and byways. It's all incomprehensible. But I guess some day I'll find it all out. Maybe some of my readers will tell me.

> Then the Pharisees went away to work out between them how to trap him in what he said. And they sent their disciples to him, together with the Herodians, to say, 'Master, we know that you are an honest man and teach the way of God in an honest way, and that you are not afraid of anyone, because a man's rank means nothing to you' (22, 15-16).

Just look at those **wily** characters. I can think of some religious orders who put me in the same situation when I wanted to have a Negro admitted to their school as an undergraduate. One of those orders sat me down, you know, like I was a queen, and then they said, "By what right do you wish us to take a Negro?" Well, I had no right, except Jesus' right. So I explained that, and then I said, "How can you keep a Negro out of here if you want to go on calling yourselves priests, nuns, and Catholics? You show ME by what right you can keep him out, and still keep the cross in your chapel!" Was I popular? I certainly wasn't! So that's how they approached him, very slyly: "Oh, you're so good, blah, blah, blah." They approached me that way, too.

> But when the Pharisees heard that he had silenced the Sadducees they got together and, to disconcert him,

one of them put a question, 'Master, which is the
greatest commandment of the law?' Jesus said, 'You
must love the Lord your God with all your heart, with
all your soul, and with all your mind. This is the
greatest and first commandment. The second re-
sembles it: You must love your neighbor as yourself.
On these two commandments hang the whole law, and
the prophets also' (22, 34-40).

Didn't they know that? I was just thinking to
myself, "We all know that." I've gone through life and
I always knew that. I try to love everybody, I really do
because of the Book. I understood that to love God is
to have faith in the impossible. Everything in our
modern world shouts that there is no God. But you
hold on to that God. Like the woman with the issue of
blood, you hang on to his robe, to his garment, and
something passes through your hands. You hang on to
that garment and a power passes through you, enters
your heart and opens it up to love everybody. That's
how it works. At least that's how I think it works.

While the Pharisees were gathered round, Jesus put
to them this question, 'What is your opinion about the
Christ? Whose son is he?' 'David's,' they told him.
'Then how is it,' he said, 'that David, moved by the
Spirit, calls him Lord, where he says: "The Lord said
to my Lord: Sit at my right hand and I will put your
enemies under your feet"? 'If David can call him Lord,
then how can he be his son?' Not one could think of
anything to say in reply, and from that day on no one
dared to ask him any further questions (22, 41-46).

Why did they want to catch him? He was so good.
And why do we always want to twist his words. I
always had to defend him.

In the laundry the power machine makes an awful
noise. All I had to do was one sleeve. This was in the
garment district in New York. All I did was the left

sleeve. Whisss! Whisss! Whisss! — the noise is terrible. Do you know that often when I read my old Gospel I hear that noise. It's the noise that Sadducees and Pharisees make. You can't hear the word of God. The noise drowns it out.

Jerusalem Admonished

Well, St. Matthew is on his way. He is quite a writer! This is chapter twenty-three, and the scribes and Pharisees are being admonished by Christ, especially about their hypocrisy and vanity.

> Then addressing the people and his disciples Jesus said, 'The scribes and the Pharisees occupy the chair of Moses. You must therefore do what they tell you and listen to what they say; but do not be guided by what they do: since they do not practise what they preach' (23, 1-3).

Now that always gets me when I come to that, because it's so clear that Christians are not practicing what they preach. It brings a terrible saddness into my heart. It really does. It seems to me that when we do not practice what God preaches we make God sorrowful.

I was just telling someone that in Russia, faced with the non-practice of charity, a Russian would begin to cry, because the greatest virtue in his mind is charity. When you go to confession to a Russian priest he asks, "Have you loved your enemies?"

Take for instance this fellow who employed me in his restaurant. He had a wife and several children. One Friday, I think it was, I was due to finish about six o'clock; another girl took over after that. He comes sidling up to me and says, "Katie, how about spending the weekend on Coney Island? Me and you having a good time!" I looked at him, and said to him,

"How about Mass on Sunday. Your wife would expect you to be there." "Oh," he said, "we could always go to Mass on Coney Island." I unpinned my apron, threw it in his face, and walked away without even asking for my pay. He was not only ready to commit adultery but he was ready to miss Mass. In my Russian heart I could see the tears. My heart cried an apology to God.

Do you remember the old days inside a Catholic Church on Sunday? You had to pay a dime just to get in. There were two little tables at the back, and two people collecting the money. The idea was to pay for your seat. In rural churches you bought a pew for the year. Our church had this custom.

Then there was the parish financial report, which listed the names of everyone and how much they had paid for their pews and how much they had given in the collection. A large sheet hung at the back of the Church. At the bottom there were some names like Smith, Brown, Jones, with one dollar or so listed for a whole year. Everybody read the report. And, of course, the Smiths and Browns and Joneses just slunk out of the church like pariahs.

But back to those characters in the big cities who collected the pew rents as you walked into the church. Where I worked in the Toronto slums the people were all Catholic but they didn't go to church. For one thing, they didn't have the money; secondly, they weren't dressed for it. You had to be decent to go to church. I said, "Look, God likes beggars." One woman answered, "God likes beggars, but not the Church." By the Church, of course, she meant the clergy and the Sisters. The Sisters were always teaching the poor kids to be decent and clean and all that. How can you be clean and decent when there is a depression on? God wouldn't mind if the church was filled with beggars!

There was something in my heart that just broke when I read that Gospel. They used to tell us what to do, but they still don't do it themselves!

Let's put it bluntly. I hate to do it but I think I must be truthful. We're fighting alcoholism. *The Reader's Digest,* which is supposed to be a family magazine, is filled with ads on alcohol, not to mention *Newsweek* and *Time.* But you understand that those people are making money out of that. Why are there bars in religious houses? I saw them myself, and one of the priests where I was lecturing said to me, "Name anything. Name your poison." Wouldn't it be simpler just to have wine on the table for everybody, like the French and Italians do? Of course, I don't judge them, but "preach and don't practice," that's the tragedy. The state of the reverend clergy and of the nuns is still (amongst the poor people) a sorrow beyond comprehension.

> Alas for you, scribes and Pharisees, you hypocrites! You who build the sepulchres of the prophets and decorate the tombs of holy men, saying, 'We would never have joined in shedding the blood of prophets, had we lived in our fathers day.' So! Your own evidence tells against you! You are the sons of those who murdered the prophets! Very well then, finish off the work that your fathers began (23, 29-32).

Jesus calls the lawyers and Pharisees hypocrites. I must admit this is a sad, sad thing. How would you like to be called a hypocrite by God? I used to muse in my little rooms, "You clean the outside of the cup" — that means always trying to look holy and good. What about the inside? Of course a lot of it is coming out with the psychiatrists, but this isn't a question of psychiatry. God can cure if we come close.

> Jerusalem, Jerusalem, you that kill the prophets and

stone those who are sent to you! How often have I longed to gather your children, as a hen gathers her chicks under her wings, and you refused! So be it! Your house will be left to you desolate, for, I promise, you shall not see me any more until you say: Blessings on him who comes in the name of the Lord! (23, 37-39).

When I used to reach this point I would fall on my knees and ask God pardon for all that had happened in Palestine in those days. For I believe — am I wrong about that? — but I do believe with my whole heart that we live in eternity. God's eternity. We come from his hand and move towards his heart. And we can pray for those who are long dead and who are in hell. I believe that we can pray for them. If Our Lady can visit hell, as the Russian legend says, then we can pray for its inhabitants. This is probably heretical, but that's the way I see it.

SIXTEEN

THE BEGINNING OF SORROWS

It's frightening, just frightening! The next section of St. Matthew's Gospel is called "The Eschatalogical Discourse." What a big word for a poor woman! Dimly I know that this big word means "concerning the last things," the last days. I understand that men have to use big words about simple things, so I let it be. I can barely pronounce it, but it's there.

> Jesus left the Temple, and as he was going away his disciples came up to draw his attention to the Temple buildings. He said to them in reply, 'You see all these? I tell you solemnly, not a single stone here will be left on another: everything will be destroyed.' And when he was sitting on the Mount of Olives the disciples came and asked him privately, 'Tell us, when is this going to happen, and what will be the sign of your coming and of the end of the world?' (24, 1-3)

This reminds me of a story. Once upon a time I was a waitress in what you call a "Greek joint," a poor restaurant run by a nice Greek fellow, frequented mostly by poor people, at the edge of the Bowery. About once a week, a chap would come in carrying a big sign which read, "The end of the world is coming." Up and down the streets he went carrying this sign, which was very tiresome.

He would come in, stand his sign against the wall, sit down, and say to me, "Katie, my feet are hurting me something terrible." One day I asked him, "Why do you carry this sign?" "Well," he answered, "I haven't got a job. I'm all alone. I don't have anybody to care for me so a dollar a day is a dollar a day."

I used to give him an awful lot of spaghetti with meat balls. A big dish! He would wink at me and say, "Thank you." And the Greek proprietor would look at me and wink too and say, "My, my, Katie, you sure give this man a very big portion. But it's okay. The Lord said we should be merciful. In my church (he was Eastern Catholic) we say 'Lord have mercy' all the time. Now here is a hungry man, and we should give him some good spaghetti. The Lord will count this for us. Okay, Katie?" I said, "Sure, sure Boss."

And I thought about Matthew. The apostles, just like us, wanted to know about the end of time. Everybody wants to know about the end of time. It's not a healthy curiosity, you know. It's kind of a slithering curiosity. I listen to that kind of question and for some reason, I don't know why, I always hear the slithering of a serpent going through the place. I guess I'm fanciful!

It's not to be marvelled at why today we think of the end of the world. Look around: the Middle East is in a state of war, practically; so is Ethiopia. South Africa is on the verge. Russia is arming itself. Do you know why Russia is arming itself? Russia is not quite arming against Europe. There's nothing in Europe too interesting for Russia. Russia is arming itself against China! That's my idea. I'm a poor woman, but I come from Russia, and we're afraid of the Chinese.

Next, Jesus says that people will be shouting all over the place, "I am Christ, and you are Christ and he is Christ, here is Christ!" He says, "Don't be alarmed." That's why I wasn't alarmed by all the Zen Buddhism and Eastern mysticism. I wasn't alarmed because I believe in what Christ says. " . . . do not be alarmed, for this is something that must happen, but the end will not be yet. For nation will fight against nation, and kingdom against kingdom. There will be famines and earthquakes here and there."

We've had many earthquakes, just as it says. But all this is only the beginning. Do you understand that? It's the beginning of the birth pangs. " . . . they will hand you over to be tortured and put to death." Many Christians already are hated. Think of Central America, South America, and the concentration camps in Communist countries.

It seems to me that the end is still far away.

Now we come to the great tribulation of Jerusalem:

> So when you see the disastrous abomination, of which the prophet Daniel spoke, set up in the Holy Place (let the reader understand), then those in Judaea must escape to the mountains; if a man is on the housetop, he must not come down to collect his belongings; if a man is in the fields, he must not turn back to fetch his cloak. Alas for those with child, or with babies at the breast, when those days come! Pray that you will not have to escape in winter or on a sabbath. For then there will be great distress such as, until now, since the world began, there never has been, nor ever will be again. And if that time had not been shortened, no one would have survived; but shortened that time shall be, for the sake of those who are chosen (24, 15-24).

Whenever I come to this part, I think of the atomic bomb. I certainly am not going to go back to get my cloak if it's radioactive. I might be mistaken, but I think that is what he foresees. Then again, he warns us that when this time comes, we must go to him and not to other prophets. This is what we're doing right now. But thanks be to God, very slowly, we're coming back to him, because the other prophets are not leading us anywhere.

Immediately after the distress of those days the sun will be darkened, the moon will lose its brightness, the stars will fall from the sky and the powers of heaven will be shaken. And then the sign of the Son of Man will appear in heaven, then too all the peoples of the earth will beat their breasts; and they will see the Son of Man coming on the clouds of heaven with power and great glory. And he will send his angels with a loud trumpet to gether his chosen from the four winds, from one end of heaven to the other .

Take the fig tree as a parable: as soon as its twigs grow supple and its leaves come out, you know that summer is near. So with you when you see all these things: know that he is near, at the very gates. I tell you solemnly, before this generation has passed away all these things will have taken place. Heaven and earth will pass away, but my words will never pass away. But as for that day and hour, nobody knows it, neither the angels of heaven, nor the Son, no one but the Father only (24, 29-36).

Here we have a picture that's rather dim. But somehow I'm not afraid. If you read this Gospel, your faith is shaken. This Gospel is like a wind that shakes the trees and all the ripe cherries (the "chosen ones") fall down. This is a Gospel of faith. It's a very difficult Gospel because it's foreboding. You wonder, you really wonder, if there is a God. You think of the atomic bomb and are tempted against faith.

I remember when Hiroshima happened. When I realized the how and why of it, I had the strangest feeling that a page of my little Gospel fell in front of me and for the first time that page cried out, "Out of the depths I cry to you, O Lord. Hear my voice, the voice of my supplication." I remember that my first reaction to the Hiroshima bomb was to enter into the mind of the person who dropped it. I asked myself, "Did that man who pushed the lever know what he was doing?

Did he really know, and then look down and see what happened to that place? He flew away, but was he *sane* after that?"

I read the newspapers and I know what's going on. The neutron bomb, the one that kills people with the minimal destruction of buildings, frightens me too. I can't explain it, but my fear grows into terror during the night. To do such a thing is murder, plain murder. That is a mortal sin. Whether it's done by a nation or by an individual, it makes no difference, it's still murder.

I see Christ in the midst of all those lethal weapons, and this is one of the horrors of my nights, of my vigils. I see Christ enmeshed in that mushroom cloud, looking out from it. We crucify Christ by dropping an atomic bomb on him. Did you ever think of that? Well, think about it! He becomes a mushroom for all to see, then vanishes, for many, forever. I don't know why I have this horrible picture, but I know with a very deep and unshakable faith that he escapes from that mushroom and enters our midst. But do you know what he does? He cries. He cries bloody tears which fall on the earth.

I used to imagine that I was at the Cross, seeing his blood fall on the earth. Looking at the earth, I thought that his tears regenerated the earth. But these bloody tears of Christ falling from the mushroom, they're like acid burning the earth! Every tear of Christ is holy. It falls on the earth which knows his footsteps. The earth can't stand it and almost gives up its soul! When the earth gives up its soul, it can't give any fruit. It becomes barren.

So when I think about this "eschatalogical discourse," I don't think of it as a discourse, nor do I think of it in such big words. I think that Christ is warning us.

I think that he is saying that man's inhumanity to man makes Him shed bloody tears.

What do I want to do? I want to wipe his tears away. That's what I want to do. That is why I am restless.

> So stay awake, because you do not know the day when your master is coming. You may be quite sure of this that if the householder had known at what time of the night the burglar would come, he would have stayed awake and would not have allowed anyone to break through the wall of his house. Therefore, you too must stand ready because the Son of Man is coming at an hour you do not expect (24, 42-44).

This is another reason why these Gospels shake me like the wind shakes a tree. I try to understand, to explain. That's why I think I have vigils. I'm always expectant, always alerted. People say I am always with God. I have to be because he might be coming, and I have to open the door, I have to feed him. He comes and he might sup with me or with all of us. We have to be alert.

This probably will sound stupid to anybody who reads this book, but I consider that we have to do some penance, some fasting, some mortification, each according to our spiritual director's advice. I really believe that penance, mortification, fasting, just might assuage the anger of the Father who beholds this whole picture. It's not an easy Gospel. I find it very hard.

When I travel — I have just recently travelled 28,000 miles — it seems to me that the pages of my old Gospel float before me all the time. In various places, in trains, in planes, they suddenly come before me. Do you know what they say? They seem to imply that I can help the Church. All these things we were talking about are reflected in the Church, and he seems to want all of us to help his Church. To help his Church is to *be* before him. We preach the Gospel by showing how we are in love with him. To *do* is next. But first, to *be* before God.

> What sort of servant, then, is faithful and wise enough for the master to place him over his household to give them their food at the proper time? Happy that servant if his master's arrival finds him at this employment. I tell you solemnly, he will place him over everything he owns (24, 45-47).

That's very clear. But today, in my estimation, there is something else going on: nobody wants to make any commitment. A few real stewards look after the Lord's goods, but the others come and go, and I'm worried about them. They're not drunkards or greedy or anything like that, but they do not stay long enough to be stewards. They disappear into a strange void where Christ is not. He's always there, of course, but they don't know it. I worry about them.

Talents

We arrive at the 25th Chapter of Matthew. I was thinking that a Communist made a movie of the Gospel of St. Matthew. It seems as if St. Matthew is quite popular with Communists and poor women. Listen to the parable of the ten bridesmaids.

> Then the kingdom of heaven will be like this: Ten bridesmaids took their lamps and went to meet the bridegroom. Five of them were foolish and five were sensible: the foolish ones did take their lamps, but they brought no oil, whereas the sensible ones took flasks of oil as well as their lamps. The bridegroom was late, and they all grew drowsy and fell asleep. But at midnight there was a cry, 'The Bridegroom is here! Go out and meet him.' At this, all those bridesmaids woke

up and trimmed their lamps, and the foolish ones said
to the sensible ones, 'Give us some of your oil: our
lamps are going out.' But they replied, 'There may not
be enough for us and for you: you had better go to
those who sell it and buy some for yourselves.' They
had gone off to buy it when the bridegroom arrived.
Those who were ready went in with him to the wedding
hall and the door was closed. The other bridesmaids
arrived later. 'Lord, Lord,' they said, 'open the door
for us.' But he replied, 'I tell you solemnly, I do not
know you.' So stay awake, because you do not know
either the day or the hour (25, 1-13).

I re-read quite often this parable of the bridesmaids. It's an intense consolation when you are poor,
especially in Harlem. At eventide, when it's almost 90°
in shade, the ladies gathered around the little balconies
of their brownstone houses, or sat on the stoops, and
sang spirituals. Sometimes they sang sad ones, like
"Nobody Knows The Troubles I've Seen." But sometimes they sang very happy ones like "All God's
Children Have Shoes." I liked "All God's Children
Have Shoes " because often the soles of my shoes were
not so very good. I seldom wore stockings. When you
walk on gritty pavements it's not very pleasant because
of the big hole in the sole of your shoe. So I would
console myself with the words of Christ. Funny that
they were a consolation to me. But they were.

"So stay awake, because you do not know the day
when your master is coming." It was hot in Harlem,
very hot. My room had no cross ventilation. If it was
95° outside it was about 105° in my room. I would
go out and sit on the stoop of the church. Father
Mulvoy would come out. He was hot too. Then I
would walk up and down a little. Then I would say to
Fr. Mulvoy, "You know, this might be the hour when
he will come. Nobody knows the hour." And Father

Mulvoy (who understood the situation pretty well) would say, "Yes, Katie, it's quite possible that he will come this hour, for no one knows either the day or the hour."

Just talking like that made you feel pretty cool. In the middle of this terrible heat, when perspiration flooded you, you suddenly got cool because he might be coming. Of course, you knew that he was in your midst, sweating too, in a sense. But that thought brought hope: "No one knows, and maybe he will come now." It was consoling, I remember that. I was no bridesmaid or anything, but it was consoling.

> It is like a man on his way abroad who summoned his servants and entrusted his property to them. To one he gave five talents, to another two, to a third one; each in proportion to his ability. Then he set out (25, 14-15).

Now, in the first place, you look at that talent and you say to yourself, "Oh, my goodness me!" I used to turn the pages of my little Bible and simply put my hands up and clap them, and say, "Oh, my goodness me, what is Christ saying here?" Let's just say that the poor guy was scared, and he stashed his talent under the tree. Well, what is the matter with Christ? Why doesn't he just forgive him, especially since he is preaching repentance all over the place?

Then I started thinking. I have been given a great talent, the Gospel. What if I went and put it under a tree, and buried it and never preached it because I was afraid of him who gave it to me? Where would the Gospel be? What would happen to it? The kingdom of God wouldn't have been preached to the poor. Can you imagine that? Just because I was a scaredy-cat! I was given this beautiful Gospel which is equal to more than five talents. I put it in a heavenly bank, and with the help of the Holy Trinity it began to fructify. Can you imagine what things would be like if the Gospel were preached to thousands of poor?

Another man had two talents; that is, he had a little Gospel. The other one had a big Gospel. What's a talent? I said to myself, "In this time a talent was a piece of money, but God wasn't interested in money. So it must be something very important. And the most important thing to Jesus Christ was that the Good News be preached to the poor. So, I said to myself, "This is what it's all about."

I'm sure that I'm untheological to the point of no return; I'm sure that I'm un-Biblical as far as scholars are concerned. But as far as I'm concerned, that's how my heart responds to it. I've been given five talents. I would sit in that brown room with the small light, and then I would get all excited. I would clap my hands and I would dance and I would say, "I have been given a huge, wonderful, beautiful gift. I must pass it on to others." And my little brown room would fill with light. Untheological, un-biblical — but I think Christian.

God continues. He speaks about the Last Judgement.

> 'For I was hungry and you gave me food; I was thirsty and you gave me drink; I was a stranger and you made me welcome; naked and you clothed me, sick and you visited me, in prison and you came to see me.' Then the virtuous will say to him in reply, 'Lord, when did we see you hungry and feed you; or thirsty and give you drink? When did we see you a stranger and make you welcome; naked and clothe you; sick or in prison and go to see you?' And the King will answer, 'I tell you solemnly, in so far as you did this to one of the least of these brothers of mine, you did it to me' (25, 35-40).

Nobody can ever know what that Gospel means to me. I always chose this Gospel to end my talks on interracial justice: "And when those who asked, 'When didn't we visit you, etc.,' (I would stop, look the audience straight in the face, and say) 'I was a Negro in America and you were white Catholics. Depart from me.'" And I would sit down. I'm telling you, it really hit those people. Some were angry; some threw rotten eggs and bananas and tomatoes and what-have-you. Others cried. Others repented. Others realized that the Negro was their brother.

This was one of the most powerful ways of preaching the Gospel that I ever had. I used the same Gospel when I preached in favor of prisoners. We used to work in all the prisons in Harlem and Chicago.

That Gospel is indelibly carved in my heart. It has eaten its way into the flesh of my heart. It's before me always.

SEVENTEEN
BEGINNING OF THE PASSION

Whenever I come to the word *passion* as applied to Jesus Christ, I rejoice because, woman-like, passion has many meanings for me. In the sense that the Gospel speaks of it, it's pain, a real passion of pain. It's a sea of pain, a Niagara of pain. It's a sea in which the waves reach sixty feet high and each one of them is a deadly wave of pain.

Passion is also love-making. Somehow I know that he underwent his passion because he loved us. There was no other reason for him to suffer it. Only a lover can enter that kind of a passion. Passion also means surrender to the Will of his Father. "Yes, Abba . . . not my will but Thine." So you see how much the word *passion* means to me.

> Jesus had now finished all he wanted to say, and he told his disciples, 'It will be Passover, as you know, in two days' time, and the Son of Man will be handed over to be crucified.'
>
> Then the chief priests and the elders of the people assembled in the palace of the high priest, whose name was Caiaphas, and made plans to arrest Jesus by some trick and have him put to death. They said, however, 'It must not be during the festivities; there must be no disturbance among the people' (26, 1-5).

I often read that Gospel. Jesus told them that he was going to be handed over and crucified, which was a manner of death common in those days, but they didn't understand. They didn't understand the conspiracy against him. They were pretty dumb, those apostles.

But then I understand why they were dumb. Who could foresee that such a Lover was in their midst? Who could understand that it was the Son of God, the Second Person of the Trinity, a bridge of reconciliation between his Father and us, between Abba and the people.

But to Jesus Christ we are not simply people. (I don't care what all those big books say!) To Jesus Christ, each one of us is precious. Each one is his beloved. He would give his life for each one of us. He would have given his life for just one person. He was the gentlest, the kindest of men, like a beautiful bird gathering all his chicks around him. There is a picture of him as a pelican surrounded by little pelicans. I always think of Jesus Christ like that. He would have died for each one! Just think of that! How precious you are! How precious I am! It used to console me, that little, little paragraph because it revealed the depth of his love.

As I grew older it seemed to me that I was entering deeper and deeper into that love of his. Some people might have thought that I was drunk at times, all alone here in this room. But I wasn't drunk at all. I was just being lifted up, or drawn down, into some deep dimension of his love. Lovers get drunk on each other.

Jesus was at Bethany in the house of Simon the leper, when a woman came to him with an alabaster jar of the most expensive ointment, and poured it on his head as he was at table. When they saw this, the disciples were indignant; 'Why this waste?' they said. 'This could have been sold at a high price and the money given to the poor.' Jesus noticed this. 'Why are you upsetting the woman?' he said to them. 'What she has done for me is one of the good works indeed! You have the poor with you always, but you will not always have me.

When she poured this ointment on my body, she did it to prepare me for burial. I tell you solemnly, wherever in all the world this Good News is proclaimed, what she has done will be told also, in remembrance of her ' (26, 6-13).

Doesn't that give you shivers? Don't you begin to realize what it's all about? The Gospel is so simple. That's why, being poor, I can understand it. You have to be poor to understand the Gospel. The more your head is filled with theology and cosmology and meta-physics and what-have-you, the less you understand the Gospel. For the Gospel has been told and written for the humiliati and the little ones. True, the rich can read it too, but they have to be simple and humble when they do that. Listen. Come with me. It's so simple.

Here were those future bishops of ours and they were yelling that this was a waste. I understand this perfectly, absolutely perfectly. When we were in Friendship House, Toronto or Harlem, "Flewy"* was really the person to watch over poverty. God knows we were as poor as churchmice, but even churchmice had something to eat. So did we. Churchmice don't die; neither did we. But I had a funny streak in me. Here we were preparing a little box of clothing for a poor woman. She gave us the size and so forth. I told Flewy that I was going to deliver it. Flewy very carefully looked for the best things for this lady because she was sick. In the meantime, I skip out and buy six oranges. And I said to myself, "She would like to have a little bit of sherry, so I'll buy some sherry." I said to myself, "She's so poor she'll never have ice cream," so I bought a brick. When I came back Flewy bawled me out! Did

---

* Grace Flewwelling, one of my most faithful companions in the apostolate.

she bawl me out! "What do you mean by getting all these things. The money can go to those poorer than she is." So I took out my little Gospel and I read to Flewy about the **anointing** at Bethany. Flewy was very holy. She said, "Sorry, Catherine. I forgot." She forgot quite often because I must admit, I did stupid things.

Take for instance that case of the social worker friend of mine. Nancy was her name. She couldn't understand why I gave so much clothing to the poor. It's because I saw how they lived. Secretly I hoped that they would sell it and get some money. Secretly. Nobody knew it. Well, Nancy walked in one day with her arms akimbo and says, "I've got you!" "You have?" "Yes, you know Mrs. S., she's on my file list." "Oh," I said, "I know Mrs. S. very well." "Do you know something? She walked right across the road to your clothing room, and according to your orders she was given ten dresses and what-not. Do you know where she went?" I didn't know where she went. "She went to the pawn shop. Do you know what she did?" I said, "No." "She sold all those dresses and went into a beer parlour. Do you know what she had?" I said, "No." "She had two bottles of beer." "Gee," said I, "I must remind the staffworker to give her more dresses so that she can have a cocktail." Exit Nancy. She slammed the door.

> Then one of the Twelve, the man called Judas Iscariot, went to the chief priests and said, 'What are you prepared to give me if I hand him over to you?' They paid him thirty silver pieces, and from that moment he looked for an opportunity to betray him (26, 14-16).

That's a very sad Gospel. You know why? Because we betray Christ like Judas did, for less than thirty pieces of silver. We betray him for a better job that we shouldn't have. We betray him for money. They said that every man has his price and it's true. Just read the paper. Each time there is a bribery of any kind — money passed under the table, etc. — you can almost hear the Sadducees and Pharisees at their marble tables. Have you ever heard the sound of silver against a marble top? I was in Greece, and that was how they count their coins. On marble. Later, when I grew up, I used to hear in my imagination the sound of silver on marble tables whenever I came across a bribery. I thought to myself, as I looked at this world, "Everybody is for sale." And so I wanted to weep.

> Now as they were eating, Jesus took some bread, and when he had said the blessing he broke it and gave it to the disciples. 'Take it and eat,' he said, 'this is my body.' Then he took a cup, and when he had returned thanks he gave it to them. 'Drink all of you from this,' he said, 'for this is my blood, the blood of the covenant, which is to be poured out for many for the forgiveness of sins. From now on, I tell you, I shall not drink wine until the day I drink the new wine with you in the kingdom of my Father' (26, 26-29).

He gave us the Eucharist! He used plain bread and wine. Whenever I think of that I want to fall down and kiss his feet. I was so poor for so long. What sustained me through all those years of poverty most of the time was just bread.

I remember when George, my son, was very little, not even yet a year old. He had to have milk. So I nursed him. But after six months or so you have to give him something else. So I used to go to the grocers and say, "Look, this is all the money I have. Would you give me enough food for my son to eat this week?" (The grocer knew George because I used to bring him in his perambulator.) He would be very generous. Then he would say, "Well, Katie, what are *you* going to eat?" And I would say, "Oh, I will eat bread." He said, "I'll give you day-old bread free of charge." So I would come back home with four or six loaves in the perambulator. That was an awful lot of bread. I would have tea or coffee with it. George was well fed. Bread for the Russian is the staff of life.

But bread is something more than the staff of life. Each time we tear a piece of bread — we seldom cut it — we think, at least I do, of an evening in the Holy Land. The air is transparent. It is twilight, but there are a few lamps already lit. He is in the Upper Room, at the passover meal. They are eating the herbs and the lamb. But it isn't the herbs or the meat that he takes in his hand. It's bread. Bread which even the beggar in the street can find.

I remember the astonishment of Dorothy Day when we were walking downtown in New York. I happened to see a piece of bread, so I bent down, picked it up, kissed it, made the Sign of the Cross with it, and put it on a ledge. She said, "What are you doing that for?" "Oh," I said, "in Russia bread is holy."

The Eucharist is such a beautiful, simple thing. Wine is cheap everywhere. It isn't cheap in America, but in France and in other countries the poor can always get wine. Wine and bread. What more does a person need to live? It seems to me that this is the food which satisfies. Everything else is unsatisfactory.

Gethsemani

Matthew continues his Chapter 26:

After psalms had been sung they left for the Mount of Olives. Then Jesus said to them, 'You will all lose faith

in me this night, for the scripture says, I shall strike the
shepherd and the sheep of the flock will be scattered,
but after my resurrection I shall go before you to
Galilee.' At this, Peter said, 'Though all lose faith in
you, I will never lose faith.' Jesus answered him, 'I tell
you solemnly, this very night, before the cock crows,
you will have disowned me three times.' Peter said to
him, 'Even if I have to die with you, I will never disown
you.' And all the disciples said the same (26, 30-35).

Strange how a poor woman enters into the Gospel
of the passion, be it Matthew, Mark, Luke, or John.
When you are very poor, you feel at home in the
Passion. It's a strange thing to say because you don't
really enter into a Passion. You either feel passionately, or you suffer passionately, or you love passionately. But I don't mean that. I mean that a very poor
woman who reads that Gospel feels at home. The
Passion is so close to the poor. Some day maybe I will
write the Way of the Cross that St. Francis invented.
You can walk the Stations, and every station reflects a
little piece of your life.

He was right in telling them that they would lose
faith in him that night. Long ago, when I was terribly
poor, living as I did in New York in the slums, I often
wondered why so very few priests came to the slums.
They were afraid. Oh, they brought the Blessed
Sacrament to the sick and the dying. But it was "No
Man's Land." Nobody ever heard much about the
priests or from the priests.

Oh, there were churches, but somehow the priests
were rich and we were poor. And though their words
from the pulpit were truly the words of God — for this
they were ordained — somehow, when they reached
us, they fell flat. They were empty. As one woman said
when we were going out (we were in the back pew

because we were so poorly clad) "Dearie, them good holy priests, they have no idea of the passion of Jesus Christ. Oh, they got their problems, but you and me, we got it in our bones." I didn't answer anything because it was so true.

Jesus said, "You will all lose faith in me this night . . . " Ever since the day I came to New York and worked in the Bowery, I knew the meaning of "the night extends." Did you ever think that "the night extends," that there is no day? There is no day because people have lost faith in him, then and now. The rich in New York didn't believe in him, not so that you could notice. At least they didn't bring forth any fruits you could see as you walked down Park Avenue.

Late one night, having coffee in Friendship House, one Negro woman who had been hired for fifty cents a day, said to me upon returning, "Sister, I look at all those people I work for and I know one thing: they sure don't know the Lord Jesus Christ." I think she was right. There were so many who didn't.

As time goes by, the night gets darker, and the words of Christ get louder, it seems to me. "You will all lose faith in me this night." Sometimes I am in my little igloo here and the night bites me. I don't think many people ever experienced the bite of a night. Yes, that's the way I feel. I sorrow, I pray here for one thing: that they don't lose faith in him all over the world. But, suddenly, as I pray, (and you know I pray earnestly, I really do, for everybody) the night turns into a lion or a tiger: it roars, it jumps at you and bites you. I speak symbolically, of course. It bites you because it doesn't want to belong to Satan. The night is his domain. And he wants people not to believe in Jesus. Sometimes I find that the night bites me.

We know that Peter did not believe in him. There

was a moment in his life when he denied him. "Then Jesus came with them to a small estate called Gethsemani; and he said to his disciples, 'Stay here while I go over there to pray.'"

As I have tried to explain, a poor woman reading the Gospel feels at home. Nobody bothers spending any time with her. Nobody cares. Sometimes I dream of a thousand brown, gray, boarding house rooms. They appear as a huge corridor in my dreams, endless, and I wander there. I'm trying to reach the end of them so as to get out. There is a door some place in my dreams, but I can never find it. I look at all those rooms, and I look at my shoes that I got from Sally Ann.

Why didn't I have any friends to share those lonely evenings in those boarding rooms? Someone to pray with me, someone to console me, someone to help me? I always believed in spiritual directors; I never was without one. But it was the hardest thing to go to a spiritual director and explain how a poor woman lived the Gospel of Gethsemani. They couldn't get it. And the strange part was that they couldn't suggest anybody with whom I could meet and share my loneliness.

I remember one time going to a church in a large city. There were many big hotels, very much like Atlantic City without the boardwalk. I worked in some of those hotels as a waitress. I was so lonely I went to the priest and asked to join the sodality. He hemmed and hawed. I couldn't figure out why he was hemming and hawing. I only asked to join the sodality. He said, "Katie, you will be much happier if you join the sodality in the next parish." I said, "Why, Father?" And I walked out of there and tried to figure it out. Fifty years later I still haven't figured it out. Why couldn't I join a sodality? Class distinction? It's not supposed to exist in America. Was nobody there of my age group? Sodality members at that time were my age group. I dreamt again of a long, long row of brown and gray rooms.

How many times did I pray on linoleum floors all over the place, prostrated as the Russians do. God kept me company. The apostles didn't keep Christ company, but he kept company with me.

"Then all the disciples deserted him and ran away" (26, 56).

When I read that Gospel I think of the year 1946. I can't say that my "disciples" deserted me. No, but they repudiated me, in a sense, for it became quite evident that *my* ideas of Friendship House and Harlem and *their* ideas were different. I read that Gospel so often. And I felt like saying, "I sat amongst you and taught you and you didn't lay hands upon me." They didn't lay hands upon me, but they believed that somehow or other I was untrue to the interracial movement, to the Negro. But I felt deep down in my heart that I had never been more true to the interracial movement, to the Negro. I felt deep down in my heart that it wasn't right for us to live only in Harlem. I knew that a page of life would soon be turned, that something would happen which would free the Negro of America a bit, and that we didn't have to limit ourselves only to Harlem. We had to open the doors of Harlem for the Negro to live everywhere.

Also I felt so very deeply called, poor as I was, to other people. Not every Negro was poor, and not every poor person was a Negro. I thought of the Rural Apostolate, to which I had been invited in Canada. Somehow or other I knew that though no one kissed me, no one betrayed me, no one did any of the things

that this strange Gospel is saying, somehow or other I
felt a kinship with it. I don't know why.

EIGHTEEN
THE TRIAL

> Then they spat in his face and hit him with their fists;
> others said as they struck him, 'Play the prophet,
> Christ! Who hit you then?'(26, 68).

Slowly the large glob of spittle descended down
my cheek. It had been ejected by a Negro who saw me
walking down the street and who stopped and spat in
my face because I was white. I let the spittle flow down
a little while I looked straight in his eyes, and I said,
"Brother, I understand why you did this to me. And it
is quite right. You vented your sadness on my face
because I'm white. You've been sold down the river by
white people so long that you couldn't stand the sight
of another white face." And I wiped the spittle off.
There was a little crowd forming around us. This big
Negro put his arms around my shoulders, kissed my
cheek and said, "Sister, I'm sorry."

Matthew continues:

> Meanwhile, Peter was sitting outside in the court-
> yard, and a servant-girl came up to him and said, 'You
> too were with Jesus the Galilean.' But he denied it in
> front of them all. 'I do not know what you are talking
> about,' he said (26, 69-70).

This is a frightening paragraph of the Gospel.
Often, in the utter loneliness of a big city, in the
loneliness of a car as I went to or returned from my
nursing calls, in the loneliness of my rooms and my
vigils, I examined my heart. Yes, I did. It's a good time
when you are all alone to examine your heart and find
out how many times you denied God. Perhaps not in

the words of St. Peter, no, but just denying him in your heart. For me, the greatest temptation came when I spoke to an audience about interracial justice. It was so easy to avoid the question of interracial marriage. They always asked, "Do you want your sister to marry a Negro?" I could have very easily answered, "The Negro doesn't want to marry *your* sister." But it would not have been true.

By the grace of God, I never denied God publicly, if you want to put it that way. But in my heart, how many times I said, "I wish I could," and the wish I think is very much like the deed. Take, for instance, God said, "If you desire a woman, you already commit adultery with her." It's the same thing about denying God. It happens in the depth of your soul.

St. Matthew continues in Chapter 27:

When he found that Jesus had been condemned, Judas his betrayer was filled with remorse and took the thirty silver pieces back to the chief priests and elders. 'I have sinned,' he said, 'I have betrayed innocent blood.' 'What is that to us?' They replied, 'That is your concern.' And flinging down the silver pieces in the sanctuary he made off, and went and hanged himself. The chief priests picked up the silver pieces and said, 'It is against the Law to put this into the treasury; it is blood-money.' So they discussed the matter and bought the potter's field with it as a graveyard for foreigners, and this is why the field is called the Field of Blood today. The words of the prophet Jeremiah were then fulfilled: 'And they took the thirty silver pieces, the sum at which the precious One was priced by children of Israel, and they gave them for the potter's field, just as the Lord directed me' (27, 1-10).

There is an interesting Russian story about two brothers who bought a field. They were happy because it was a good field. They plowed slowly with their horses, and as they did, now one, now the other, would find a piece of silver. They were so astonished. At the end of the day they brought it to the house and showed it to their wives. There were thirty pieces of silver. The wife of one came in; she hadn't seen it yet. He put his hand out to show her, but he couldn't pick the silver up. Each piece was so heavy that he asked his partner to help him, but he couldn't pick it up either. The pieces of silver had some kind of inscription written on them which the brothers didn't know.

They looked at each other, and they decided that the best thing to do was to put some holy water on the money. So they put some holy water on it and immediately the pieces of silver were light again. They got a linen bag and rushed it to the priest. The priest was a learned man and he said, "This silver is from the period of Pontius Pilate. These are Roman coins, the kind that the Jews and the Romans used for taxes and trade."

Suddenly he fell on his knees. "That's the money they bought the bloody field with! That's the money they paid for Jesus Christ!" Everybody fell on their knees. The priest began to tremble, and kissing each piece, blessed it with holy water and his own blessing, then put it back again into the linen bag. Rumor had it that he took it to a monastery. He made a whole journey through Odessa to the Holy Land and he brought it to St. Catherine's Monastery. And that's where it is to this day, so they say. But, of course, it's only a legend.

Matthew continues:

The chief priests and the elders, however, had persuaded the crowd to demand the release of Barabbas and the execution of Jesus. So when the governor spoke and asked them, 'which of the two do you want

me to release for you?' they said, 'Barabbas.' 'But in
that case,' Pilate said to them, 'what am I to do with
Jesus who is called Christ?' They all said, 'Let him be
crucified!' 'Why?' he asked, 'What harm has he done?'
But they shouted all the louder, 'Let him be crucified!'
Then Pilate saw that he was making no impression,
that in fact a riot was immanent. So he took some
water, washed his hands in front of the crowd and said,
'I am innocent of this man's blood. It is your concern.'
And the people, to a man, shouted back, 'His blood be
on us and on our children!' Then he released Barabbas
for them. He ordered Jesus to be first scourged and
then handed over to be crucified (27, 20-26).

A poor woman, as I said before, enters the
Passion from the inside. Her ears hear the Greek or the
Latin tongue, the Aramaic or the Hebrew, and her
heart reverberates with the terrible noise that the
people make with the shout "Barabbas." This word is
forever imprinted on her mind as if with a bloody
stamp. Poor people know pain only too well, although
they haven't experienced the terrible pain Christ had to
experience in being beaten up and crowned with
thorns. It seems to me, anyhow, as I read my old, old
Gospel, that I was inside the Passion of Jesus. And all I
could do was cry. Huge, silent tears fell down my
cheeks no mater where I was. For I understood that
this was the price he paid for me.

Christ Is Mocked

The governor's soldiers took Jesus with them into the
Praetorium and collected the whole cohort around
him. Then they stripped him and made him wear a
scarlet cloak, and having twisted some thorns into a
crown they put this on his head and placed a reed in his
right hand. To make fun of him they knelt to him
saying, 'Hail, king of the Jews!' And they spat on him
and took the reed and struck him on the head with it.

And when they had finished making fun of him, they took off the cloak and dressed him in his own clothes and led him away to crucify him.

Above his head was placed the charge against him; it read, 'This is Jesus, the King of the Jews.' At the same time two robbers were crucified with him, one on the right and one on the left (27, 27-38).

Well, that's a very tragic Gospel. Strangely enough I read and re-read it, and always I read it when I had great heaviness or sorrow. I don't want to say "problems" because I was never problemless, but when I had seemingly insoluble situations. I would sit on a chair, open this Gospel, and read it. I would read, and it would be etched on my mind forever and forever. They disrobed him and they put a red cloak on him and they spat on him and they made fun of him. They put a crown of thorns on his head. Then they drove the thorns into his head, as deeply as possible.

And I said to myself, "That is what's happening to me." I remember a time when money was desperately needed for my son. He was very young then; three or four years old. And also for my mother. She was a refugee from the Communists just like all of us, and she went to Belgium. Cardinal Mercier was very kind to my brothers, giving one a high school education and both of them a university education at Louvain.

My mother lived in Brussels in a little flat, just a room and a kitchenette. She had a coal stove. In the Fall she would go down the hilly street to the coal merchant's who lived below the little hill. She would fill the buckets and painfully carry them back to her room. When I was in Belgium I used to help her. The buckets were heavy even for a young person. How did she earn her money? She got what they called a peddler's cart. She collected newspapers and medicine

bottles. In those days pharmacists paid a few pennies
for old or used medicine bottles.

She would start her rounds in the morning.
People were kind, putting out newspapers just by the
door, and she would collect them. She would sell the
newspapers to the man who bought them. (I don't
know what he did with them but they were in demand).
She would collect the medicine bottles and bring them
to a certain pharmacist who paid her about two
Belgian cents per bottle. She made a few francs that
way and that helped her a little. I never talked much
about my mother.

One day I heard from my brother that she had
been ill, and would I send some more money. I couldn't
send her very much when I was in manual labour, but
whenever I could spare a dollar I would send it. When I
got the letter from my brother I realized, yes I did, that
I too was naked. When you get menial wages in the
'20's you are naked.

And everybody makes fun of you too. You are a
dirty Polack, a dirty foreigner. Day in and day out
these words enter your heart like little stilettos.
Because, it's really obvious that everybody is making
fun of you, or at least those people who call you by
those names. So sometimes I felt as if I had a crown of
thorns. It was in those dark and despairing days when I
was trying to find a job and couldn't get one.

But back to the letter of my brother. So my
mother needed a little more money. I had a job as a
waitress, what they call "a lunch job." You came about
11 a.m. and you worked eight hours. But I could also
nurse, so I applied to a private hospital which catered
to rich people who had babies on the QT. I worked
there at night. I left the hospital at 7 a.m., went home,
slept a little, and at 11 I went to work at the restaurant.

I got a little tired.

But it brought me money which I was able to send to my mother. So I said to myself, "Yes, there are times when we human beings carry the crown of thorns that Christ had." Maybe it's lack of sleep when you have to moonlight. Maybe it's just a sort of a depression that goes with it. I wouldn't know. But whenever it happened, I read that Gospel again and again. Not because it was Lent, or because it was near Easter, or because in the churches the Passion was celebrated. No. I understood that I was a church too because I was baptized and the Trinity dwelt in me. So I could call myself a church. Perhaps it was stretching theology, but somehow or other I knew that those who loved him had to go through what he went through. And since I couldn't go to church due to the lack of time, I seemed to be a church myself. After all, she's his Bride, and because she's his Bride and she loves him, she suffers with him. Just like his mother suffered with him. And she's the prototype of the Church. So I read that Gospel at various times of the year.

> The passers-by jeered at him; they shook their heads and said, 'So you would destroy the Temple and rebuild it in three days! Then save yourself! If you are God's son, come down from the cross!' The chief priests with the scribes and elders mocked him in the same way. 'He saved others,' they said, 'he cannot save himself. He is the king of Israel; let him come down from the cross now, and we will believe in him. For he did say, "I am the son of God."' Even the robbers who were crucified with him taunted him in the same way. (27, 39-44).

Yes, they mocked him and I always felt that so many people in history mocked him.

I remember when I was seventeen or sixteen. I read a book by an author called Renan, in which he mocked Christ. And I remember reading that book and kneeling down and asking God to forgive him, even though he was long dead probably. I felt so very strange when people mocked Jesus Christ. It seemed to me as if I were in a crowd, and the balmy air of the Holy Land was softly playing with my hair. I was there, and I heard them mocking, especially the priests. Then the laity, of course, mocked him. But somehow I didn't bother so much about them because they had to mock him if they professed to be atheists.

But every time I looked at them, so to speak, with the eyes of my mind and my heart, I saw such a big chasm between their lips and their heart. They mocked him with their lips, but their heart kept saying, "What if he *is* God? What if he *is* God?" It was a question on their faces. Stalin had it. Lenin had it. I'm sure lots of Communists have it now.

But the ones I was fearful of, and from whom I wanted to run away, were those who made *obeissance* to him. It said in my little poor Gospel of a poor woman, that those soldiers knelt and called him the king of the Jews. *Obeissance* means "bowing down." Those were the ones that I was afraid of. With them, things were reversed: Their hearts hated him and yet they made obeissance to him. Hypocrites, the ones that he himself denounced. "You hypocritical generation!" I fear those people very much, for they seduce many people by their appearance of bowing, appearing to worship him whom they crucify every minute.

Now take, for instance, those who do not pay fair wages, those who take away the bread of the poor, those who buy the Third World's raw materials at cheap prices and sell the finished products at a high price. I fear the merchants of war, the ones who are selling and buying nuclear devices, airplanes and the rest of it, and yet go to church on Sunday. I fear them, and in my poor little rooms I was really sorely afraid. Of them and for them. The pain of Christ at that point really engulfed me. And I would look at the Gospel there, my shabby little book, and I would put my head on its pages and I would cry. Cry for the crucified Christ, cry for those who mocked him. Cry for the hypocrites. I realized that they crucify him all the time — even now.

> Next day, that is, when Preparation Day was over, the chief priests and the Pharisees went in a body to Pilate and said to him, 'Your Excellency, we recall that this impostor said, while he was still alive, "After three days I shall rise again." Therefore give the order to have the sepulchre kept secure until the third day, for fear his disciples come and steal him away and tell the people, "He has risen from the dead." This last piece of fraud would be worse than what went before.' 'You may have your guard,' said Pilate to them. 'Go and make all as secure as you know how.' So they went and made the sepulchre secure, putting seals on the stone and mounting a guard (27, 62-66).

It was such a foolish thing to do, I thought, when I read my Gospel in my brown room. You would think they were modern police. They put seals on the stone! When the police today want to seal a room they also put seals across the door. It's all so funny, for where does it get you? You cannot seal Christ away in any tomb. But do you know what happens? Your *heart* becomes a tomb. You run around looking for something to seal it with so that he should never come up again and bother you. Lots of people are in that state, looking for sealing wax to seal Christ in their heart so that he never comes out.

How many youngsters come to Madonna House and say, "I don't believe in the resurrection of Jesus

Christ." Recently I was reading one of those intellectual magazines in which there was question of his resurrection. Theologians, and all kinds of philosophers and psychologists, filled page after page after page. I read it all. In my little Gospel I re-read what is said here and said aloud to the night, "The fools! They think they can put a stone before his tomb and seal it!" Can you imagine that? Well, I feel really sad for all those people. Just plain sad. Because who can seal in God? Tell me.

Usually, I have a very lovely thought when I think about this Gospel. Isn't that funny that in the midst of this tragedy I have a lovely thought? Yes, I think of a different kind of seal: "Set me like a seal on your heart, like a seal on your arm" (Song of Songs 8:6). Isn't that beautiful?

> Meanwhile the eleven disciples set out for Galilee, to the mountain where Jesus had arranged to meet them. When they saw them they fell down before him, though some hesitated. Jesus came up and spoke to them. He said, 'All authority in heaven and on earth has been given to me. Go, therefore, make disciples of all the nations; baptise them in the name of the Father and of the Son and of the Holy Spirit, and teach them to observe all the commands I gave you. And know that I am with you always; yes, to the end of time' (28, 16-20).

I was always disappointed with Matthew's ending. I like St. John's account a little better where he shows Jesus preparing breakfast for them, and walking through a closed door, and the whole story of Thomas. I like that. Matthew is brief. He doesn't want to go into all that. I bet you he was too shaken to write it all out. Especially after a few years. The whole thing must have sort of snowballed. You know how it is when you look back. It gets more and more awesome. So he made it simple.

I like the sentence, "And know that I am with you always; yes, to the end of time" (28, 20).

Now that really pulled me through! Sometimes I thought I was in hell when I was so persecuted in Harlem and Toronto. It was like hell. And I would re-read that part of Matthew and say, "Well, strange as that may seem, I, a refugee, a stranger in a strange land as I always call myself, I have been chosen to preach the Gospel in my own way. How do I know I have been chosen? Because I am persecuted. When you are persecuted you are like Jesus Christ and so you are supposed to do what Jesus Christ did."

I had many tragedies in my life, but they became stepping-stones to my faith. And as they multiplied they formed a stairway. In my little back rooms of Madonna House and Friendship House, whenever darkness fell upon me like a cloud, always in the distance, at the top of this stairway, I could "see" Christ beckoning me saying, "Come on higher, friend. Come on higher."

other writings by
Catherine de Hueck Doherty

Apostolic Farming
Dearly Beloved -- 3 volumes
Dear Father
Dear Seminarian
Doubts, Loneliness and Rejection
Fragments of My Life
The Gospel Without Compromise
Journey Inward
Molchanie
Lubov
My Heart and I
My Russian Yesterdays
Not Without Parables
Our Lady's Unknown Mysteries
Poustinia
Re-entry into Faith
Sobornost
Soul of My Soul
Stations of the Cross
Strannik
Urodivoi
Welcome, Pilgrim

Available through Madonna House Publications